Letters t

Your Handbook has made my life a treasure I never dreamed possible.

J.K., New York

How does one thank someone for the greatest gift ever received? My life was stuck. It was like being in deep mud. I was afraid. I was lost. Now I am free! I have done what it was that you wished for me in your I Ching Handbook: I have "mounted to the skies of success as though on the wings of six dragons." I did it! And it's a brand new world.

M.L., Sioux City, Iowa

I have just purchased copies of The I Ching Handbook for my daughter and her husband. Considering what it has done for me, it may be the greatest gift I have ever given anyone.

H.K., Federal Way, Washington

God bless you, *wu wei*, for your I Ching Handbook! I was skeptical when I bought it, but in three months I have overcome a fear that has plagued me since childhood and I am joyful, truly joyful, for the first time in my life. I am now 63.

R.L., Bangor, Maine

Walking the path of the I Ching Handbook has been the greatest event of my life. I'm a new woman. Words can't express what I feel. I wish everyone could share this great adventure.

C.M., Miami, Florida

Because of the incredible changes I made following the path in the Handbook, I purchased a copy for each of the 40 employees in my company. Many of them have told me of the wondrous change it has brought to their lives.

A.L., Newport Beach, California

I want to thank you for what The I Ching Handbook did for my father. He bought it two months ago, and since that time, our lives have changed for the better almost beyond description.

K.Y., Louisville, KY

It's true! It's true! It's true! Bless you, *wu wei*.

L.L., Pittsburgh, Pennsylvania.

It was tough, real tough, but I did it! Now I feel as if I can do anything. And the truth is, I probably can. My career is off like a skyrocket, my life has blossomed, I'm in love, and I'm riding high! Thank you a million times over.

M.P., Des Moines, Iowa

The path was right there in front of me all my life and I never knew it! I live in a brand new world! My parents never knew how to help me, my teachers never knew, and neither did my friends. Walking the path in the I Ching handbook gave me happiness, control of my affairs, and FREEDOM.

H.W., London, England.

I didn't believe it when I read what the book claimed it could do, but I hoped, I hoped real hard, because I've never been what you would call a powerful man, but I didn't really believe it. Here it is, two months after I began "The Path," and I'm here to tell you that it is the God blessedess thing that's ever come down the pike! It works! I live in a brand new world that was right there in front of my eyes all my life and I never seen it until I walked *wu wei*'s path. *Wu wei*, you are the bomb!

S.F., Grand Rapids Michigan.

It says in the Bible, "I was blind, but now I see." I never really knew what that meant until I followed your path in the I Ching Handbook. The world is a different place for me now. Much different. I never had much, but now I can have what I want. I never knew I was powerful, but I am! I always thought I was a woman in a man's world, destined to take a back seat. Now I'm in the driver's seat! God bless you, *wu wei*, whoever you are.

Z.B., Raleigh, North Carolina

What can I say? It works! And of course, thank you!

T.T., Ft. Worth, Texas

The hardest part is getting past regretting the time I lost before I walked "The Path." I'm 83, now, and finally, I "see."

W.W., Vancouver, British Columbia

THE I CHING HANDBOOK

GETTING WHAT YOU WANT

By *wu wei*

Power Press

Los Angeles, California

The I Ching Handbook

GETTING WHAT YOU WANT

By *wu wei*

Power Press,1310 Riviera Avenue, Venice, CA 90291
Telephone: (310) 392-9393 Fax: (310) 392-7710.
Website: www.power-press.com
Email to *wu wei*: wuwei@power-press.com

Library of Congress Card Number: 99-60537

ISBN: 0-943015-31-6

First Edition

10 9 8 7 6 5 4 3 2

Other books by *wu wei*:

THE I CHING

THE BOOK OF CHANGES AND HOW TO USE IT

I CHING WISDOM

GUIDANCE FROM THE BOOK OF CHANGES

I CHING WISDOM, VOLUME II

MORE GUIDANCE FROM THE BOOK OF CHANGES

A TALE OF THE I CHING

HOW THE BOOK OF CHANGES BEGAN

I CHING LIFE

LIVING IT

I CHING READINGS

INTERPRETING THE ANSWERS

THE I CHING WORKBOOK

A LIFETIME WORKBOOK

THE I CHING

PC COMPUTER VERSION

50 YARROW STALKS

Hand gathered by farmers in northeast China specifically for use in I Ching divination

Publisher's Statement

THE I CHING HANDBOOK is a book of great and powerful change. Because it is based on the I Ching principals of Universal law, it can bring tremendous change to your life.

Those of you who are familiar with *wu wei*'s other books will find that this book is quite different in style and form from his other books. *wu wei* wrote this book for those who want more control over their own destiny, for those who want to lead more powerful and productive lives, and for those who want to experience the wondrousness, the joy, and the inexpressibly supreme essence of life that is possible in our Universe. If that is you, welcome.

***wu wei*'s comment**: "Because you are reading this, be aware that the Universe, in its complete awareness, has brought you together with what you need. It means you are ready. I wish you the courage to make the decision to go forward. Have faith in the way the Universe works. This path is a wonder-filled journey, but very difficult, and your determination must be great if you are to complete the path. Leave skepticism and doubt behind. Open your mind. Allow yourself to believe. The rewards are everything you want them to be. I am with you every step of the way on this most wondrous journey."

wu wei's message

Many years ago when I first began my I Ching studies, I became aware that there were Universal laws. Many years later, I became aware that several of the laws formed a path one could follow that led to the achievement of goals. I followed that path until I was sure of it, achieving the goals I set for myself, then led others who had unfulfilled goals along the path. Their goals were varied: some wanted homes or cars or other physical assets, some wanted financial security. A great many desired a loving relationship that would endure. Some wanted to be free from dependencies, and yet others sought to find work that they loved. A few were searching for peace, and others for power. Some sought for enlightenment.

I always asked everyone why they wanted whatever it was that was that they desired. The answer was always the same: "Because it will make me happy." Everyone was seeking happiness.

Many had crippling fears that prevented them from accomplishing their desires. Most just didn't know how to get what they wanted or how to be truly happy. All had one thing in common that prevented them from having what they wanted: they had developed beliefs that were inconsistent with Universal law. Acting on the basis of what they believed brought results that were inconsistent with what they desired.

In every case, those who followed the path to the end were able to achieve their goals, overcome their fears, and have what they wanted. Most importantly, they discovered who they were in relationship to the Universe, and what that meant. It allowed them to perceive a brand new Universe—a treasure chest.

Now it is your turn.

Whatever you now do, whatever you now believe, whatever your current circumstances may be, you are perfectly equipped and fully capable of fulfilling your needs and desires.

You can have what you want.

I humbly offer you my assistance in the form of this book and the accompanying disk. I wish you great good fortune. May you mount to the skies of success as though on the wings of six dragons.

-wu wei

Beginning The Path

The I Ching Handbook
is the guidebook
that will lead you along
the path.
It is made up of
***concepts**,*
***stories**,*
instructions,
*and **exercises**.*

The stories
are examples
of the concepts
in action;
the instructions put you on the path,
and the exercises
provide you with a way
to put the concepts to use
immediately.

Part of the information in
The I Ching Handbook
is written in the form you are now reading.
That was done
to increase your understanding
of the individual sentences
and to make easy
the assimilation of the information.

There are some people who,
for various reasons,
cannot
or do not
follow directions.
If you are one of those,
this is a ***perfect*** *time*
to change that.

This is an ancient path,
a narrow path,
and
there are only a handful
who walk it.

Not following directions
will cause you to miss the path,
and you will find yourself
where you were
when you began.

To achieve success on the path,
it is ***essential***
that you carry out the directions
precisely*:*

FIRST INSTRUCTION

Read slowly.
Give your mind time
to ***fully*** *absorb the information.*
Speed reading
will cause you to miss part of what's here.
I understand that you are eager to have what you want,
justifiably so,
but thoroughness is
required.
Therefore, if you find
you have read a paragraph, or even a sentence
quickly,
relax, and
read that part again.
Make certain
you understand
every sentence
in this book.

Sometimes we read words with our eyes
that we fail to understand with our minds.
The words in
The I Ching Handbook
call for
your **full** *understanding.*

SECOND INSTRUCTION

Several hours after reading a chapter,
glance through the pages again;
Make a note to yourself ***now*** *to do that later.*

Please forgive the following redundancy,
but I want you to succeed.
In the preceding paragraph
you were asked to make a note.
If you did that,
congratulations!
You are correctly on the path
and ready to proceed.
If you did not make the note,
please do so ***now***
as this is the time of beginning.

In *I Ching Wisdom, Volume I*, it is stated:

> *Exceptional enterprises cannot succeed*
> *unless the utmost caution is observed*
> *in their beginnings.*

wu wei's comment:

In the beginning of even small things, exceptional care must be exercised if a planting is to lead to a flowering. How much more then should exceptional care be exercised when great or dangerous undertakings are begun? A flaw, built into the beginning, increases with time, and if not corrected, will ultimately cause the failure of the enterprise. The superior person can always see the end in the beginning; he knows the seeds and, exercising great care, enjoys a lifetime of success and good fortune.

THIRD INSTRUCTION

Review preceding chapters.
This renews
and increases
your understanding of the concepts.

Each time
you read a previous chapter,
the concepts will become clearer
and you will discover
different *meanings*
and ***new*** *information.*
The clearer the concepts become,
the more capable you will become,
and the sooner you will bring about
having what you want.

Only do the exercises
the first time you read a chapter.

Walk the path of
The I Ching Handbook
*with your **full** effort.*
Become so familiar with its concepts
that they become part of you.

React to life
as described within these chapters.
Then
you
will
find
what
you
seek,
and you will find it
marvelously
and abundantly better
than you have ever imagined.

(The instructions will no longer be numbered)

It has taken you as many years as you've been on earth
to become the way you are
and to obtain what you have.
Because the way you are
and what you have
is different from,
or less than
what you want,
you need to make some changes:
***Basic** changes;*
***Inner** changes.*

The moment you were conceived,
you began storing information
in your memory.
It now contains everything
you've ever
read,
heard,
seen,
imagined,
and experienced.

Even though you may not recall
everything,
it is all there,
stored away.

Everything
you now perceive
is sifted through your memory
to see how it fits
with all that has gone before
so you can determine how to act upon it.

Following the path
In
The I Ching Handbook
will provide your memory
with new information
that will cause you to act differently
as your future unfolds.
That will naturally bring about
new
and different
results:
being who you want,
having what you want.

Chapter One

First Step On The Path

Communication

Talking with the Universe

It is of ***utmost*** *importance*
that you become aware
that you
and your Universe
are in ***constant*** *communication.*

Of the three or four
most
important items of information
that exist on earth,
that *is one of them.*

Some of us
communicate knowingly,
others of us
unknowingly.

We speak to the Universe
with our words,
thoughts
and actions.
the Universe speaks to us with
***events**.*

Events
are the language of the Universe.

An example of that communication
is what we call
"coincidence."

A coincidence
is generally thought of as a
chance happening;
an unplanned occurrence.

*It is **not** that.*
There is nothing
"by chance"
in our Universe.

All
is
by design.

If you believe in "chaos,"
meaning "random chance,"
or "complete confusion"
the I Ching could not work.
But the I Ching
does
work.

If chaos **could** *exist,*
which is the
only *environment in which*
chance **could** *exist,*
the Universe would have destructed long ago.

If chaos existed,
the continuation of the Universe
would depend on chance, a flip of the coin:
Heads,
continuation,
tails,
discontinuation.

Surely by now,
in the trillions of years gone by,
tails
would have come up
once.

When we
fully
grasp the concept,
that the Universe is
one of absolute order,
and alive,
aware,
and
in ***constant*** *communication*
with us,
and
we with it*,*
our lives take on
a new meaning
and a new potential
that makes all that has gone before
pale
into insignificance
and brightens our futures in limitless ways.

We become happier,
more confident,
and less afraid
because *of our knowledge.*

We
consciously
become partners
with the Universe;
consciously
an extension of it;
consciously
a part of it.

As you proceed on this path,
your awareness
of your communication
with the Universe
will grow,
and you will experience
a relationship
with your Universe
undreamed of.

Right now,
***as you read this**,*
The Universe,
is communicating to you
through the words on this page.

*They are **exactly** what you need,*
right now.

Further Communication

The Mirror

The world around you,
its people, places, objects, and events,
is a mirror.
It shows you
"Who You Are."
It is of major importance
that this concept
be fully understood
and clearly pictured in your mind.
The following examples will assist you
in doing this.

Imagine a woman
whose mind is very precise and ordered.
Imagine that she is intelligent,
neat in her habits,
friendly, hard working,
and honorable.
If you saw her home
it would be neat,
clean, cheerful,
nicely furnished,
comfortable,
and in good repair.

You would see
"Who She Is"
mirrored there.
If she performed a task,
you would see her mirrored in her work -
it would be well done.
If you met her friends,
you would hear
"Who She Is"
mirrored in their descriptions of her.
Everything about her,
the way she carries herself,
the way she dresses,
the words she speaks,
her actions,
all mirror
"Who She Is."

Imagine that we looked in on the life
of another woman who had many of the opposite
characteristics of the first woman.
Her mind is not precise or ordered,
she is not very intelligent,
she is lazy, sloppy in her habits,
unfriendly, and dishonorable.
Her life would mirror
"who she was."

If you saw these two women together for a day
you would see the remarkable difference between them,
the world communicating
"Who they are."

Suppose you purchase a small item.
The change you receive from the salesclerk
is five dollars too much.
Your immediate reaction,
whether you keep the money
or give it back,
and how you feel about your actions later,
all mirror
"Who You Are."

Suppose you have just won a race;
imagine all the excited spectators,
cheering, shaking your hand,
congratulating you.
They are all
mirroring
your victory.

Suppose you had won
the same race,
but you had cheated.

Suppose some of the spectators knew it.
Their angry protests,
their hissing and booing
would clearly mirror
"Who You Are."

It is important that you understand
that the world around you
is ***constantly***
and ***immediately***
communicating with you
by
mirroring,
" who you are."

With that understanding,
you will ***use*** *the mirror*
to make changes,
to take responsibility for
your image
in the world's
mirror,
and
to change your image
to one you
admire,
respect
and love.

That image
will make your life a joy.

In the book,
I Ching Wisdom, Volume II
it is written:

"We create the world by our expectations.

Wu wei's comment:

Thinking the world a selfish place, we find selfishness. Selfishness is what we look for, what we expect, and **consequently**, what we find. Having found it, we say to ourselves, "I knew it." Thinking the world a generous place, we find generosity."

That is another way the world mirrors
our thoughts and beliefs.

So, the concept
you are to form in your mind is -
the world is a mirror.
You are to now look at
your current circumstances:
your physical condition,
your possessions,
the conditions in which you live and work,
and the situations surrounding your life,
as mirrors
showing you
"Who You Are."
Put the book down,
take a few minutes
and do that ***now****.*

As you continue on this path,
you will see
everything *around you changing,*
mirroring
your changes.

Many years ago, I gave a series of workshops designed to break people loose from that which held them back from having what they wanted. The people made such wonderful changes, such dramatic changes, that soon I was asked to do a number of radio and television interviews. Several days after I had been interviewed on a radio show, a man named Ralph telephoned to say he had heard the show and wanted to know more about the workshop I was holding at that time.

We talked for a while about the various situations in his life: his work, which he disliked, his marriage, which seemed a continuous quarrel, his home, which was a small, poorly furnished apartment, his family, which was too large for his income, his few possessions, and his lack of control over outward circumstances.

He asked where the workshop was held, and when he estimated it would be a one hour drive each way, he said, "Gee, that's tough! I don't think I want to do that."

I replied as gently as I could, "Ralph, the drive to the workshop is easy. Keeping your life the way it is—that's tough."

This "mission of change"
you are on
*is **tough** to carry out.*
*But, what's **really** tough*
is to live the rest of your life
lacking what you truly want.

The changes you are going to make
in order to have what you want
*are **interna**l changes.*
Having made them,
your outward circumstances will change.
It will be the world
mirroring your changes.

If you want to see everything in the world
colored yellow,
you can either
*get **a lot** of yellow paint*
and a brush
and start painting,
or,
you can put on yellow sunglasses.

Changing ***the way*** *you see things*
is ***much*** *easier*
than changing the things you see.

When you put on yellow sunglasses,
the whole world becomes yellow
instantly.
The moment you make internal changes,
the outside world changes
instantly.

The circumstances you need
to make these internal changes
are ***already in place****,*
part of your life,
and will emerge as
"work out situations."
Because of what is currently in your memory,
you might still see them as
"problems,"
but your job
is to recognize them
with
"new sight."

After a lifetime
of seeing problems
as bothersome,
troubling difficulties,
the change to seeing them
as beneficial work out situations
will be a welcome one,
and a difficult one to make
but . . .
you ***can*** *do it.*

It may be difficult for you at this time
to believe that the problems
in your life
are there
purely
for your benefit,
but
it is so.

In later chapters,
you will learn concepts
that will enable you
to handle these
"work out situations,"
more easily,
but for now,
it is enough
that you develop your awareness
to the point where you can see
problems,
difficulties,
and obstacles
as
"work out situations."

The principles that govern physical power
also govern mental power.
Body builders achieve their powerful bodies
by working out,
"pumping iron,"
which means they lift heavy weights
over and over again.
There's a saying among body builders -
"No pain, no gain."
That means
if you're failing to use your muscles
to the point where they hurt,
you're failing to build new muscle tissue.

The situations you need
to work out on
***will** be difficult.*
By using your efforts
to overcome the difficulty,
you'll build mental strength,
gain awareness,
and increase your capability.

***Welcome** difficult situations.*
Resolve to face obstacles
rather than to side-step them.
*That **is** an act of courage,*
and
*the rewards are **wonderful**.*

Believe
that problem situations arise
purely for your benefit.

How do you "start believing"?
When a problem
or a difficult situation arises,
say to yourself
***as if** you believed it,*
"This is for my benefit."

Your beliefs,
like everyone else's,
are based upon your experiences -
on what you know.
By pretending and acting
*as if you **truly** believed it,*
you'll soon discover
*that it **is** true -*
***then** you'll believe it.*

In the beginning,
if you encounter a major problem,
you're likely to react by saying,
"This is for my ***benefit****?*
That's impossible!"

The major problem has a meaning:
It means ***you are ready*** *to make*
a ***major*** *change.*
Congratulations.

I will tell you a secret:
Even the worst outcome you can imagine
is
totally
for
your
benefit.

It is ***very*** *difficult to keep aware of that piece of information,*
and even more difficult to believe it,
but once you believe it,
and
keep aware *of it,*
the world will be a ***totally*** *different place*
from the one you now know.

*We **are** the Universe,*
a part of it.

Our Universe,
*being **completely** aware*
*of our **every** action,*
and
knowing
we have started on this path,
provides us with
problems
*of **exactly** the right size*
for our growth.
*They are **never**,*
too big,
too complicated,
or beyond our control.

Most of the time,
when a difficult situation arises
we see it only
*for what it **appears** to be,*
and fail to see it
for what it really is: an opportunity for benefits—
benefits of self awareness
and personal growth.

Suppose an event takes place
in which you are involved
and it is stressful to you in some way.
How you react during and after the event
reveals you
to yourself.
It is a mirror.

After the incident is over,
if you could sit quietly
and watch a video tape of what happened,
you would learn a lot about yourself.
If each time you went through a situation,
you were to view a video tape
several hours later to see how you had behaved,
it would only take a little while
before you went ***through*** *each new situation*
behaving in a way that would please you
when you saw the replay*.*

It's important
that you keep in mind
that when the path gets tough,
you're still on the right path,
just a tough path.
Your job is to proceed as described.

I met Caleb Usher and his wife, Susan, many years ago, when they were twenty-three years old. Caleb was a fairly good carpenter and did odd jobs. He had a winning smile, a good disposition, and a boyish attitude that people liked.

Caleb's and Susan's relationship suffered because of Caleb's lack of assertiveness and general weakness. Consequently, there was unhappiness, bickering, and quarreling mixed in with the good times. The one small room they shared in the back of his parents' house was hardly a peaceful existence because of the considerable traffic through it to the garage and the backyard.

Caleb and Susan had difficulty paying their bills and their credit cards were always at the maximum limits. Their spending was always "out of control." Their possessions were a few pieces of furniture, the tools Caleb used for his carpentry, and their two heavily financed cars.

In those days, their lives were characterized by an inability to have things the way they wanted them and an overall instability. Other people and outside events controlled them. Caleb felt locked in by his meager earnings and powerless way of life. His struggle to maintain his credit and back room lifestyle was somewhat less than successful. Caleb told me of an incident from his childhood that summed up his general way of being.

In Caleb's neighborhood there lived three tough boys who liked to push Caleb around. Since he was afraid of them, he let them do it. One day, one of the boys wanted to have some fun by beating him up. I remember Caleb telling me how the blood spurted out when this one boy finally punched him on the nose and broke it.

Caleb told me that after the incident, he enrolled in a karate class and in four years learned how to defend himself well. I asked him if he had any more trouble from the boy who had broken his nose.

"No, after the boy broke my nose they left me alone, and that's all I ever wanted from the beginning."

Caleb thought he had learned a valuable lesson: "how to win by losing."

Shortly after I met Caleb, I asked him if he would like to radically alter his lifestyle by following an unusual training path. I told him it would be a difficult path and a long one, and because of all that had gone before in his life, there was a possibility that the effort would be too great and he would quit. After a long discussion about the path, he agreed to make the effort.

Almost immediately, the first "work out situation" arose. Caleb's wife, Susan, a blonde, suntanned, native Californian, was delightfully attractive and drew the attention of many men. Caleb was lost in knowing how to deal with that. One day he came to me in a distressed state.

"A man sent Susan a negligee with an invitation that said, 'Let's get together.' When she put it on, you could see right through it! I could tell she loved it."

Caleb was hurt and distressed by Susan's reaction. His "win by losing" lessons had poorly prepared him to handle the situation.

I told Caleb that it was a perfect work out situation, hand tailored to bring about the best result possible. I told him to go to Susan and ask her to give him the negligee, then to find the gift giver and return it to him, telling him that he, Caleb, was the only one who could give his wife such an intimate gift. He was to do all this in a straightforward, non-aggressive, but assertive manner. As you can imagine, that was a radical change from Caleb's usual "it's okay to push me around" attitude. Although Caleb is of average height and physically fit, he was frightened. I asked him to call upon his courage, and I described what might occur if he failed to act - his wife, losing respect for him, might accept the man's invitation! Caleb acted. He went to Susan and asked for the negligee and the name of the gift giver so he could return it along with his demand that the man never do such a thing again. Susan was thrilled! Her timid husband was being manly - and over her! She cooperated fully.

Caleb telephoned the man, identified himself, and asked for his address so he could come and see him. The man, sensing Caleb's determination and wanting to avoid any possibility of a meeting with an angry husband, refused to tell Caleb where he lived. Caleb attempted for three days to find him but the man had stopped answering his phone and had an answering machine taking messages. Caleb left many messages, all of which went unanswered. Susan was excited by Caleb's bold and unusual behavior and treated him like a king. Caleb realized that Susan was mirroring the change in his behavior. He loved it!

Gradually, ever so gradually, he began to see that the way he drove a nail into a piece of wood was connected to the way he signed his name on a piece of paper, that the way he took care of his tools was connected to the way he spoke to Susan, that getting to work on time, every day, was connected to walking, which was connected to being a good friend, which was connected to how he drove his car, which was connected to paying his bills, which was connected to waking up with a smile, which was connected to eating, which was connected to being fit, which was connected to sleeping, which was connected to playing, which was connected to having . . . all that he wanted. He began to see that everything was connected to everything else.

Three years after Caleb started the path he owned over one and a half million dollars of real estate with good, solid equity, including his own home. He drove his own, fully paid for Mercedes and had two other cars as well. He truly amazed everyone who knew him as the insecure, incapable, "weak kid on the block."

Making It Yours

Exercise Number One.

"The events that occur in my life are 'work out situations'. They enable me to see who I am and to grow in awareness and capability."

Memorize the above statement, write it down on several pieces of paper. Carry one with you, paste one on your mirror, put one on your dresser, take one to school or work, place them where you spend time. Bring this thought to mind in your day-to-day affairs. Keep at it until you automatically say to yourself when an event occurs that needs handling, "This is a work out situation designed perfectly for me to see who I am and to grow in every way."

Exercise Number Two.

See yourself as-if-from-a-distance during an entire day and keep in control. That means that when you become aware that you're awake, even if your eyes are still closed, look at your mental state and take charge of it. Realize that it's a "just right" day for you, regardless of what you're going to do that day or the problems you have. Keep aware of your thoughts while you're brushing your teeth, getting dressed, and during your other daily routines: see them as mirrors. During the day, naturally bring out your best abilities. Look at everything you do as if you were looking in a mirror. Radiate good will, cheerfulness, and well being in your contact with people - see them as mirrors. Treat them in a way that causes them to mirror you in the way you want to be seen. Be aware during stressful events that they are simply "work-out situations." Keep aware of what you are feeling, how you are acting, and what you are thinking.

An event may seem personally very important and you may get "caught up in it" and forget to be aware that you are to be "looking at yourself." If that happens, go back over the event afterwards. Mentally view yourself, see how you acted, how you felt, what you thought. Each event is a mirror - Use them to become aware of "Who You Are".

When you can say that you have spent **most** of one day being aware of yourself and "who you are," and that you kept aware that the events of that day were "work out situations," you may consider this exercise completed. Be certain you have spent **most** of one day keeping aware. Anything less is short of the goal.

Even when this exercise is completed for the purpose of going on to the next chapter, you are to keep aware, as described, every day of this path. That is the path, your path. Follow it well and **bring the change about.**

Exercise Number Three.

Choose a small task that needs to be done - **something you've been putting off**. Choose a simple task, because you are going to fulfill it **to your complete satisfaction**. That means you are going to do it **as well as you can**. It might be putting your desk or closet in order, patching up a hurt friendship, straightening out a misunderstanding, or improving a situation. One reader who had recently moved into a new apartment chose getting the whole apartment in order as her task; that was too hard because it would take weeks to accomplish and that is not the goal of this exercise. Another reader chose delivering some clothes to the cleaners on her way to work as her task; that was too easy. Be thoughtful in making your choice. The perfect task is right there as part of your life.

Avoid setting time goals such as, “I will finish my task by tomorrow at 5:30 p.m.” If you set a time goal for tomorrow at 5:30 p.m. and fail to meet your deadline, you will have failed irreversibly in meeting your deadline. The amount of time it takes to accomplish your task is the least important consideration in this exercise.

As with the beginning of all things, the beginning of your task is of great importance; focus your attention fully and keep aware that you are following the path that leads to what you want. Complete your task with care as it prepares you for all that is to come, which is more than the rest of this path - it’s the rest of your life.

The finishing of the task you choose is an important symbol of completion, but what is equally important is **the process** of doing it. Do it well and **to your complete satisfaction**. Use your full determination in bringing about its fulfillment.

Your task is also a workout situation, so observe yourself as you go through it. See if you work cheerfully or crossly. See if your attitude in completing the task is one of eagerness and anticipation in being on a new path of self-development that leads to what you want, or if you are doing it as a chore to get over and done with. **Your attitude in completing your task is as important as completing it**. If you finish your task haphazardly or in a sloppy manner, you will be far from ready to continue on the path. You may believe that you are already a fairly accomplished person and performing this small task satisfactorily is well within your capability, and therefore, you might be tempted to perform this exercise only passably. Reconsider! When you come to have what you desire, you will want to be **completely** satisfied. You are now getting to know how to bring that about. **Complete satisfaction is on its way to becoming a central feature of your life.**

When you plan to finish a task "to your complete satisfaction," it often takes on a whole new aspect. Simply getting a task done and out of the way may only take a short time. The same task, accomplished "to your complete satisfaction," may take ten times the effort and time.

You are starting to build the strengths which, when fully developed, will enable you to reach every goal. If events occur that get in the way of accomplishing your goal, that's just right. By overcoming them, you will build the strengths you need for other and greater accomplishments. The steps needed to be taken by you to get to the next level of your development are part of the framework of your life; they are perfectly suited to you.

After you have chosen your task, turn to the page at the end of this chapter headed "My Task" and write down what you chose for your task and the date. Also, write anything you want in describing your task. During and after the fulfillment of your task, write any comments about yourself that you observed while performing the task.

Be thoughtful in choosing your task, but having chosen, fulfill your task knowing it is mirroring your every thought and action. Your finished product is an expression of "Who You Are." You will probably become aware as you are doing your task that it is doing you as well. The better you do the task, the better it does you. Polishing a wooden table until its exterior surface gleams, polishes your interior surface until it gleams. Completing that task perfectly prepares you to complete any task perfectly. That is the path.

Exercise Number Four

You are to spend **most** of one day being aware of the "obvious" communications from the Universe to you. For instance, if you are expecting an important telephone call and are away from the telephone for almost the entire day, but receive the call during the one time you are near the telephone for a few minutes, acknowledge the Universe in some way such as with a knowing smile or quietly saying, "Thanks," is enough. If you are looking for a parking space and one is there waiting for you, acknowledge the Universe for it. If you meet a friend you haven't seen for some time, or meet someone that is of benefit to you, or meet someone who you had been planning to see but hadn't, acknowledge the Universe for it. If you find something you lost, get something unexpected and pleasurable in the mail, become aware of something beautiful, have a plan work out, be unexpectedly successful at something, acknowledge the Universe for it. The Universe, in it's infinite knowledge, knows of your path, knows that you're looking for the communication, and will provide more obvious communications. You're job is to simply acknowledge them. Even though, for the purpose of completing this exercise, you are to keep aware for the **most part of one day**, keeping aware of that kind of communication is something you will do your whole life. It is the most rewarding dialogue of which I know. Remember that you are to keep aware of the communication for **most** of one day. Less than that does not fulfill the exercise.

Exercise Number Five.

A major goal of this path is that you be able to experience happiness, joy, ecstasy, or whatever you feel when doing something that gives you pleasure. Therefore, you are to enjoy a half hour of pleasure.

Perhaps you'll choose walking in the hills, on the beach, or in a favorite park. Perhaps you'll go to some favorite spot and sit and read. Maybe there's a film you want to see or a friend you want to visit, but if the film you see or the friend you visit disappoints you, **then pick another pleasure exercise**. If you allow problems or other unpleasurable thoughts to intrude and spoil your half hour of pleasure, **either start over or choose another pleasure exercise**. If, in fulfilling this exercise, you take a day off to go somewhere, or take a weekend trip, then while you're away, set aside a **special** half hour to fulfill this exercise. Giving yourself pleasure is an art that can be learned. When you are finished with this path you will have acquired that art.

The way to begin this exercise is to say aloud, "I, (your name), give myself permission to enjoy a half hour of pleasure." Say that now, if this is the start of your pleasure exercise. The second step is to decide what your pleasure exercise will be. The third step is turn to the page at the end of this chapter headed "Pleasure Exercise Number One," and write what you have chosen along with the date.

When you have completed your pleasure exercise, write a brief summary of what happened, how you felt, and any other special thing you care to write. If you had to choose another pleasure exercise because one was spoiled by an unpleasant event, write that also. Be thoughtful in what you write. Many years from now what you wrote will give you much pleasure.

"My Task"

Date:

Date Completed

“Pleasure Exercise Number One”

Date:

Date Completed

Complete the exercises before going on to Chapter Two.

Do not read ahead.

Do not leaf through the book

Keep aware that you are on a magical journey

Complete the exercises with good humor, high spirits, and laughter in your heart.

Follow the path precisely to reach your goal.

Chapter Two

The Perfect You

(Remember to read slowly)

The enormous amount of energy it takes
to create a
conscious being
is almost beyond imagining.
The following is what it might be like.

Imagine the earth
with all of its mountains, oceans, and plains,
its forests, jungles, and deserts,
condensing,
becoming smaller.
First to half its size,
then to a quarter of its size,
and then to the size of North America.
The earth in its smaller size
still weighs as much as it did originally,
it has only compacted.
As it compacts
it generates enormous energy
in the form of heat and light.
It glows hotter and hotter,
brighter and brighter.

Now,
imagine the earth with its remaining,
already compacted mass,
squeezing down to the size of a ball
a hundred feet in diameter.
Think how dense it would be,
how heavy.
A teaspoonful of this compacted earth
would weigh trillions of tons.
Imagine the earth
condensing still further
to the size of a tiny grain of sand.
As it condenses
it generates incredible heat.
It glows and radiates like a tiny sun,
but far more brilliantly.
Imagine this tiny grain of sand
continuing to shrink,
until suddenly,
it ceases to have substance at all
and births into **another dimension**,
a dimension that lacks form,
but is still "held together"
by a kind of tension.
We'll call it "Consciousness."

This Consciousness
is aware of itself.
This awareness
*is what makes it a "**being,**"*
a perfect being.
That is an idea
of what it might be like.

In order for this perfect being
to gain experience
on the physical plane
it needs a physical body.
The opportunity for this occurs
when the male sperm
joins the female egg.

However it comes about,
you are a vast collection of energy,
able to create,
to move,
to think,
to do.
In the entire ***known*** *universe,*
we,
on this planet,
are the only ones
who have achieved this wonderful consciousness,
this ***awareness****,*
this being-ness.

Because
the awareness
of your perfect being
is absent at birth,
and because,
as you grow,
you learn through trial and error,
you believe
that you sometimes do things
in the wrong way,
that you are less than perfect.

Your body and brain
go through a training period:
they learn how to walk, run, throw a ball,
speak, sit, stand,
write, read, and move about in life.
They learn many lessons;
some well,
others poorly,
but ***you are always***
a perfect being.

You've been told
that you make mistakes
but,
the person speaking
failed
to
tell
you,
each time*,*
"You are a perfect being,
learning to use your body and brain,
which is done by practice,
and,
in practicing,
you'll make mistakes
and you'll seem to fail.
But, you are ***always*** *a perfect being."*

You might feel
that you are less than completely well spoken,
less than completely capable,
less than completely good looking,
or that you lack other qualities
you think desirable.
However,
you are still a perfect being.

Electricity
is a form of perfect energy.
Imagine it operating through a faulty machine.
The electricity still retains its perfectness,
its essentially pure nature and energy form,
but it ***appears*** *to be*
"working improperly."
You,
as a perfect,
radiant being,
are operating through a physical body
that is less than 100% efficient,
less than 100% trained.
You may ***appear*** *to be*
"working improperly,"
as when you make a mistake,
become ill,
have a physical impairment,
or ***seemingly*** *fail.*
But,
you are *a perfect being.*

Your physical self
is the substance
your conscious-being self collected
so it could gain physical experience.
Any thought that you are completely defined by it
is false.

The moment your brain became functional,
you began to build an image of
who and what
you believed yourself to be.
All the events of your life
have helped to create that image.
It is
"Who You Think You Are."

Perhaps a parent told you,
from the time you were very young,
"You're wonderful and I love you."
The words remain in your memory,
supplying you with that information.
Each time someone is critical of you,
the words of your parent are there:
"You're wonderful and I love you."
It is a fortunate child
who receives this kind of positive image building.

Perhaps when you were five years old,
you were given a new toy
which you broke shortly after receiving it.
Perhaps the parent
who gave you the gift
came in and saw the toy broken and exclaimed,
"You're so clumsy!"
Perhaps that criticism hurt you;
perhaps you thought about it a lot.
Afterwards, when you dropped something
or hurt yourself,
perhaps you thought,
"I'm clumsy."
Many years pass
and you've forgotten the original incident,
but the words are there,
feeding you from a subconscious level,
saying,
"I'm clumsy."

Imagine for a moment
that when you were in the second grade,
you were attracted to the child
with the soft brown eyes.
Imagine that you
went over to the child,
very shyly and timidly,
and said,
"Would you like to eat your lunch with me?"
And the child replied,
"What!
Eat my lunch with a creep like you?
I'd rather eat my lunch with a toad!"
You crept back to your desk,
hoping you were the only one
who had heard the remark.
The embarrassment and hurt impressed itself
upon your mind.
You began to form an image of yourself
as seen through the eyes
of the person who made the remark.

It was probably a long while
before you made such an attempt again.
Imagine the next time,
perhaps years later
and with a different person.
You may have said something like,
"Ah, well, um, I, ah, was wondering
if you would like to ah,
maybe, um, well, you know,
eat your lunch with me?"
Perhaps the person laughed at you
and jeeringly said,
"No Thanks!"
The image of yourself
that you had formed from the first experience
helped to create *the second response*
and was now reinforced and solidified.
After two such harsh, image-forming events,
it is doubtful that
you would have made another attempt for many years.
Perhaps by that time,
the two events had faded from your memory,
but the image they created
was still feeding you from a subconscious level,
still influencing the way you acted,
still being a part of
"Who You Think You Are."

So, here you are,
a perfect, radiant being,
operating through a brain
that has been programmed
with at least some of the following limitations:
"Into every life some rain must fall,"
"You can't have your cake and eat it too,"
"You've got to take the bitter with the sweet,"
"You can't have it your way all the time!"

The radiant being, who you truly are,
is always complete and fully present,
but the body and mind that it operates through
has clouded its radiance,
dulled its brilliance.
It is covered over by layers of false images,
misconceptions, and accepted flaws.
After a while,
the outer covering -
the ***seemingly*** *real you -*
seems to be the ***only*** *you.*

To give your perfect being
the freedom to express itself clearly,
you are now going to clear that perception in your mind.

While you're awake,
your brain ordinarily functions
at thirteen to thirty electrical cycles per second.
Researchers call it the beta level.
Sleep occurs
when your brain is functioning
at seven to eight cycles per second.
As you lie down to prepare for sleep,
your breathing slows,
your heart beat slows,
and consequently,
your brain cycles begin to slow.
Just before you pass into the sleep stage,
while your brain is functioning
at eight to twelve cycles per second,
you experience a marvelous flow
of thoughts, ideas,
and creativity.
This relaxed, slowed - down state
is called the alpha level.
At that level you are more receptive to suggestions.

Your body and mind
react to an imagined experience
in much the same way
that they do to an actual experience.
When you're hungry and think about food,
your mouth waters.
When you imagine a piece of chalk
making a squeaky sound on the blackboard,
you get a shiver up your back.
When you close your eyes and imagine yourself
walking on a tight-rope across a deep canyon,
you experience some of the frightening sensations
that you would experience ***actually*** *doing it.*
Having gone through a heavily impressive experience,
you can remember it years later
and again experience
some of the same feelings and emotions
that were present originally.
At the alpha level
you can imagine very powerfully
and your mind is also very receptive
and, therefore, your imaginings will be very effective
in producing the desired result.

The conscious journey to the alpha level
is a pleasant experience.
Once you are there,
***everything** is as you imagine it to be.*

You are now going to journey to the alpha level
where you will use your imagination
to create your life as you want it to be.
You will also meet your "perfect image,"
and experience that image
with your conscious mind.
This will help you see yourself
the way you exist
on the "perfect image" level.
That means
*you will see **all of yourself** as **perfect** -*
your physical self,
your career self,
your social self,
your student self,
and all the other selves that make up you.
You will bathe the part of your mind
that is your "every day consciousness"
with these images of your "perfect being."

In the beginning,
you may have difficulty
seeing your perfect image;
that's all right,
it will gradually appear
in later sessions.
Begin by seeing yourself
as you would ***like*** *to look.*
If you would like to be slimmer,
or have longer hair,
or wavy hair,
or be taller,
or wealthier,
or be in top physical condition,
in your imagination,
see yourself that way.

As you experience
the journey to the alpha level,
allow yourself the luxury of letting go -
give yourself up to the experience -
allow yourself to flow with the words
as you hear them

Let your imagination have full reign.
At first
that takes a high degree of concentration
because thoughts of the day
may intrude into your thinking process.
Consciously push those thoughts aside
and keep your attention fixed
upon what you are hearing.

At the alpha level
you will see things in a certain way.
***However** you see them*
is correct.
If, for instance,
you hear that you are to imagine golden stairs,
then whatever kind of stairs,
in whatever shape you imagine them,
is correct.
They can be spiral or straight,
round or square.
They can rise quickly or slowly.
***Whatever** you see is correct.*
If you hear that you are to imagine a pond,
the pond can be as wide as a street,
or as wide as a football field.
***Whatever** you see is correct.*

Making It Yours

Exercise Number One.

Carefully cut the perforation on the plastic envelope at the front of this book (about 1 inch from the top of the envelope) and remove the CD. You can store your CD in that envelope. To begin this liberating, revitalizing, transforming journey, find a comfortable seat, and relax. Do not lie down, as you will most likely fall asleep. If you do fall asleep, that's all right, because you will still hear the information. In later sessions, you will remain awake. After you have finished your journey, come back to this page and read on.

Wasn't that wonderful? If you experienced any difficulty in seeing your perfect image or in visualizing any portion of your journey, that's all right. In future sessions you will see everything as you wish it to be.

The journey you have just taken is a valuable asset in becoming who you want to be and in bringing about what you want to have. When you bathe your conscious mind with the image of your perfect being, your conscious mind becomes saturated with the assets, virtues, and powers of your perfect image. Your perfect image is all-powerful, has 100% integrity, and is one with eternity. As the weeks pass and you become familiar with your perfect image, you will naturally and effortlessly begin to act **as** your perfect image. When you're talking to another person, doing a chore, or engaged in other activities, imagine yourself as your perfect image and allow yourself to act in that manner. By being "Who You Are," you will bring about a new reality for yourself. The universe is **required** to respond to you as you are being at every moment. "Who You Think You Are" is changing as you follow this path. Let that happen. Allow yourself to believe you are the extra special person you meet in your imagination. By experiencing your perfect being, you will bring that being to the surface of your life and everything will be different for you: far better, far brighter, far easier, far more possible. "Who You Think You Are" is now going through the same kind of change a caterpillar goes through to become a butterfly. The image you hold in your mind of "Who You Think You Are," has been around since the day you were born. Your "perfect image" has been around since the dawn of time. It is as bright and as fresh and as powerful as the first brilliant day of the universe. It is all-powerful. It is you.

Take the alpha level journey once a day for thirty days. Then, let one week pass without doing it. Repeat that schedule for three months, taking the journey once a day for thirty days, then letting one week pass without taking it. Mark your calendar **now.** After three months you may continue to take the alpha level journey once a day if you want to. Taking the Alpha Level Journey once is enough for the purpose of completing this exercise.

Exercise Number Two.

Find a comfortable place and sit quietly for a half hour. Let your mind wander back through your past, remembering three seemingly unfortunate events that you have experienced. Spend some time thinking about what happened. Then, see those events as though they were **completely** beneficial to you. In the beginning you may have to pretend, but your job is to keep seeing them as "perfect," as "just right" for you. Think of later events that gave you pleasure and hook them together in your mind, realizing that the good events were part of the **same** "chain of events" as the unfortunate events. If you give up, you'll be giving in to feelings of despair and despondency, and regret, and all you'll get is - despair, despondency, and regret. Treat yourself to some good feelings. If a half hour is too short to accomplish this, take longer, or use several half hour sessions.

By changing the way you feel about past events you will change the past. The events may remain the same, but how you feel about those events will change. The events that are now causing you emotional hurt or anger are to be looked at in a new way, a way that will cause you to have good feelings about them. To feel frustration, anger or other hurtful emotions is to carry a burden. Who is it who would willfully carry a burden? Know that you know you have **chosen** to feel the hurt, the emotional pain, or the anger, and let it go. Replace those feelings with good feelings about what happened. **Free yourself**. Complete this exercise before going on to exercise number three.

Exercise Number Three.

Enjoy another half hour of pleasure. Begin by saying, "I, (your name), give myself permission to enjoy a half hour of pleasure." Fulfill this exercise outdoors unless the weather or other circumstances prohibit it. Make this half hour special. Pamper yourself, treat yourself as a perfect being. At the end of the half hour, if you find that it has been less than pleasurable, start over or choose another pleasure exercise. After the exercise is completed write a brief summary on the page headed "Pleasure Exercise Number Two." Be thoughtful in what you write so that you can obtain the maximum benefit from your experience.

Complete these exercises before going on to Chapter Three.

“Pleasure Exercise Number Two”

____

Date Completed

Chapter Three

The World of Perfect

Many years ago I went to Kauai, one of the Hawaiian islands. Kauai is known as the "Garden Isle" because it is lush and tropical - an exquisite jewel. I had been preparing myself for the trip for some time with fasting and mental preparation because it was my plan to go on a "vision quest," which is an American Indian ritual. The Indians use the ritual to reach states of heightened awareness, to discover their true Indian names, to find their missions in life, and to receive information of a spiritual nature helpful for the fulfillment of those missions. Ordinarily, at the start of a vision quest, one goes alone into the wilderness, dressed only in a loin cloth or naked, and equipped only with a knife. After several days, lack of food and shelter combine to bring about a state of heightened awareness. To naturally reach such a state is one of the great experiences life has to offer and I have sought and found these experiences in many ways. I had been mentally and physically preparing myself for this vision quest for months and my state of awareness was already quite keen.

My friend, Tom, who lives on the island, was my guide to the various sites of tropical splendor. Every time we came to a new place, he would laugh and say, "The next one's better!" Finally, we came to a high cliff and looked over the edge, straight down into the Pacific Ocean. "I saved the best one for last," he said.

Everything I saw was a shimmering, glistening, spectacular panorama of beauty. "Tom, this is exquisite!" I exclaimed.

We walked a short distance to a new vantage point which overlooked a small valley with a winding stream that gurgled and laughed and sparkled on its way to the ocean. In the valley was a farm planted with healthy, vibrant vegetables and bright flowers that nodded their heads in every direction. During our tour of the garden Tom said, "This is nice, but the really best part is further down where the land meets the ocean!"

It was hard to believe there could be a better part. We walked along a path that followed the stream and soon came to an area where the trail meandered around the side of a hill, revealing the mouth of the stream. The small cliff over which the stream plunged was crescent-shaped and the water looked like melted glass as it fell fifteen feet into the tidal pools below. In the tidal pools swam fish of every description. Slightly to the north was a tiny peninsula with a crevice running from the tip, back to the cliff where it widened into an underground cave. The waves plunged into the crevice and ran it's entire length until they disappeared under the cliff wall and then smashed into the back of the cave with a pound and a roar that shook the earth. Further out and slightly to the south was a jut of rocks that pushed their way into the ocean about a hundred and fifty feet. The U-shaped lagoon created by these two arms of land seemed alive as the shimmering aquamarine water rose and fell with the waves. It was one of the most beautiful places I'd ever seen.

"This is paradise!" I exclaimed.

Tom said, "This little farm belongs to me, and I want you to come here and visit anytime you like."

It was as if St. Peter had just opened the pearly gates. I planned my first visit for the very next day.

That opportunity fit in perfectly with my plan to experience a small portion of my vision quest.

The next morning, I set out equipped with a seven foot spear for underwater spear fishing, a fish hook and line, a knife, and high hopes. The day was magnificent! The sun shimmered on the ocean, the waves were calm, and the breeze gentle.

I was quite alone as I made my way down to the tidal pools, took off all my clothing, and with my spear, began the walk that would take me to the tip of the rocks and a most unusual and enlightening experience. Walking naked on the rocks and holding my spear caused me to feel very primitive and vulnerable. It took about ten minutes to reach the tip of the jut of rocks. From where I was standing I could see a considerable distance in every direction and from the mountains at the center of the island to the ocean at my back, it seemed as if I was the only person on the island. Visually, there was a complete absence of living souls, ships, planes, houses, and cars. The only sign that a human had ever lived on the island was an old lean-to built on the side of a hill, barely visible through the trees.

I was filled with energy and excitement. My body felt taut, my stomach muscles flat and hard, my thighs and legs powerful. I felt light and springy. My shoulders and chest were swelled with power and my eyes saw clearly. The light was superb and the air felt sharp and alive. The ocean breathed gently against the shore. My bare feet, used to shoes and sidewalks, felt a strong awareness of the rock I stood on. A sound came from deep in my throat, drawn by the great primal force of "All That Is," which is what I call the universe and the consciousness that flows through it. My body tensed as exhilaration filled me. I felt very exposed out there on the end of the rocks and unusually alive and excited. I began deep breathing and focused my attention on being a part of it all. I tensed the muscles of my body. I felt the air moving the hair on my arms and legs, I saw the brilliance of the sun as it flashed on the water, I felt the fine spray from the ocean as the waves broke, and my being responded with an air of urgency - an "opening" as when the sun's rays fall on a flower.

I knew from my reading how to proceed - the four directions each had a gift for me and I was about to begin the ritual to receive those gifts! Grasping my spear in both hands and raising it above my head, I faced north.

"I salute you, great direction of the North, and receive your gift of wisdom!" I cried aloud.

It was a strange sensation to be standing there with a spear raised over my head, shouting into the wind. It felt powerful, unusual, awesome, and a little embarrassing all at the same time. I experienced a rush of adrenaline and my mind seemed to clear even further. My vision sharpened and my other senses intensified. I felt alive and aware in a way I had experienced only at other times of unusually heightened awareness. I turned a quarter turn to the right and again raised my voice.

"I salute you, great direction of the East, and receive your gift of illumination!"

My body tingled; I had goose bumps on my chest and arms. I felt a surge of power rush through me! The spear felt alive - like some great antenna. I turned a quarter turn again.

"I salute you, great direction of the South, and receive your gifts of trust and innocence!"

"All That Is" responded! Waves crashed, the wind picked up sharply, the forces around me intensified and I turned a quarter turn for the last time and my voice flew over the land.

"I salute you, great direction of the West, and receive your gift of inward looking!"

I remained standing with my spear raised, experiencing a rush of excitement that made my heart pound! It is at times like these that the veils that cover my "inner vision" fall away and there, in my mind's eye, is a truth I've been searching for. It's like looking at a page of dots, some darker than others, knowing they form a picture, but failing to see it. Then, one day, the picture you've been searching for leaps out at you in sharp clarity and you wonder how you could have ever failed to see it. And once seen, it is then impossible to see anything else!

And so it was for me on that crystal clear morning at the tip of the rock jetty in the Pacific. My nakedness, the strangeness of the ritual I had performed, the vastness around me, the aloneness, the months of mental and physical preparation, and my previous times of heightened awareness, all caused the concepts for which I had so long sought to form in my mind's eye.

I realized then that all I had experienced up to that point in my life, the ordeals, the barriers, the impediments that I had seen as obstacles, the joys, the exhilaration's, and the achievements, were but preparation for that moment and what was to follow.

The wind was blowing my hair, the sun was warming me, the exhilaration was carrying me, carrying my thoughts to places loftier than I had ever experienced before. All feelings of strangeness and exposure were gone. I felt secure, relaxed and natural - at home in my universe. The realizations of the way things are and can be, formed in my mind one after the other:

I live in a universe
where the law of cause and effect is absolute.
Stated, the law says:

Every action produces a result,
and the result
is in perfect accord
with the action.

"I am a primary cause.
I produce effects
that agree with and reflect how I am being
at every moment."

"I am the center of my personal universe."

***"Every** event that occurs*
is perfect -
it is also
the only possibility."

*"**Every** event that occurs*
provides me
with the greatest possible benefit."

*"**All** things are possible*
for those who believe
that all things are possible."

*"I am a **perfect** being -*
***everyone** else is too."*

"The Universe
*is in **constant** communication with us*
and we with it."

"Separation is an illusion;
*All **is** one."*

*"It is **always** now."*

I walked back to the tidal pools and looked for a long time into the water, thinking of the wonder-filled concepts that had now crystallized in my thoughts. They had been forming for many years, and now that their certainty was upon me, I felt grateful. I was happy and contented in a special way because the truth, as I perceived it, was the realization of my fondest hopes. I was happy in the knowledge that I lived in a perfect universe and that I was part of it, as much as the galaxies, the trees, and the earth.

I thought, "I am here, at this wondrous moment in time called 'now,' which is the **only** moment anyone can experience, and I am gifted with these most wonderful concepts, and I now can live by them."

I was hungry from my long fast and decided to catch a fish. I tied a fish hook to a line and then tied a stone to the line for a weight. I pried some bait off the rocks with my knife and put it on the hook, then whirled the rock around at the end of the string and cast it out, but as I loosed the string, the hook lodged in my finger and the stone shot forward, pulling the hook sharply into my flesh causing blood to spurt out. Pain shot up my arm. I looked at the hook sunk into my finger and I spoke aloud my instant reaction: "Perfect!"

The crystallization of the concepts I had perceived that day was due, in part, to an intense desire I have to live in a world where **everything** is perfect. I **want** to believe that we live in a universe where **everything** is for our **complete** benefit. I **want** to believe in a **perfectly** balanced, **perfectly** ordered universe where, even though I am a tiny part, I **am** important - **and you are important**. And the Universe is completely aware of me, and of you, and will not let anything bad happen to us. And more than just important - that we are **special** beings, able to direct our own courses, able to evolve spiritually to higher planes of existence, that our spirit has a personality and that the personality survives, that we **are** eternal. I **want** to believe these things and, as a result of my wanting, I continually search for evidence that supports the way I want things to be. I have found the evidence and, therefore, I **do** believe them. However, because the universe continues in a moment-by-moment unfolding of always new events, it is necessary to always be acknowledging the rightness, the perfection, of those new events. The "wanting to believe" is what keeps me nodding my head in agreement.

"So," I thought, "at that spot in my finger is an acupuncture point that needed piercing. Since everything that happens to me can only be in my best interest and the best possible event, everything concerning this "accident" has to be perfect!"

I laughed aloud, feeling another surge of energy sweep through me. The new concepts were already working! Look what they had just done for me - it took a nasty event and turned it into something that increased my awareness and exhilaration. There I was with a fish hook sunk into my finger, feeling good about it!

The fish hook in my finger symbolized my passage from a world where pain, caused by an isolated, unlucky event, could put an end to the pleasure of a moment, to a world filled with an endless variety of experiences whose temporary and sometimes unpleasant effects were all united in a single purpose: A perfect and necessary now.

Fortunately, the barb of the hook had not gone into my finger, and I reached out and took hold of the shank of the fish hook and pulled it out. When it came out it hurt a lot, but my appreciation of the moment continued and all I could do was rejoice in my good fortune. I rinsed my finger in the ocean and sat down to think about the events of my life that had led me to that moment.

I recalled a time when I was in Naples, Florida, which borders the Gulf of Mexico. The sunsets are spectacular, and one day as I came to the gulf, I was treated to an unusually brilliant blaze of color. Clouds were towering thousands of feet in the sky, like muzzle blasts from cannons. The sun had splashed their edges with intense reds, oranges, and yellows, highly accented by white and silver. Streaks of light had broken through the clouds painting the ocean. I remember thinking, "This is a perfect sunset!" A day or two later, I came again and saw yet another spectacular light and cloud show and I realized that it, too, was a perfect sunset. "They're all perfect!" I recalled thinking. And, of course, every sunset that ever was and ever will be is a perfect sunset. Some are more spectacular than others, some are just gray, leaden skies, but they are all perfect.

A year later, I was filming on the Pacific Coast in Big Sur, California, at the top of Pfeiffer Rock. I was operating the camera and had just moved the focus of the lens from the face of the actor down to the ocean, a hundred feet below. A big wave was building five hundred yards offshore. I let the camera run as the wave built and grew, and built some more. Spindrift was blown from the top of the wave, creating shimmering rainbows in the air as the wall of water rolled in toward shore. Finally, the wave crashed with a great resounding roar against the rocks, rocketing spumes of water high in the air. "Perfect!" I thought to myself. I looked out to the ocean and there appeared another wave, just as beautiful, just as big, just as spectacular. "And of course, just as perfect," I thought. "All the waves that ever were and ever will be are perfect."

The pain in my finger soon subsided and I spent the rest of the day swimming, sunning, and feeling as good as I had ever felt to that point in my life.

Late that night, at the house where I was staying called "Hale Moana," the "House by the Sea," I wrote the following:

The absolute test
to determine if something is perfect
is:
If it happened—
it is.

The degree to which you can align yourself
with that thought
is the same degree
to which you will have aligned yourself
with your universe.

By giving your **total** *agreement*
to what has happened
at every point in time,
you have harmonized yourself
with
"what is."

Can you reverse time
and cause an event
to undo itself?
What is,
simply "is,"
*and **all** you can do,*
without exception,
is to react to it,
by either
liking it,
or
disliking it.

If you feel you are a victim,
or have had bad luck,
or have made a mistake,
or have been ill-used,
you can curse your luck,
become angry,
or feel frustrated.
The events
that have caused your feelings
are beyond your power to alter,
even a little bit.
*What **can** be changed*
are your feelings.

If you look at what has happened
as being perfect,
you will feel better in viewing the events of your life,
even accidents
and apparent tragedies.
You will be able to go forward,
in step
with your universe.
You will come to know
that when an ***apparent*** *mishap occurs,*
you will soon know
its purpose,
its necessity*.*

You will see
that what happened
is a contribution
to the continuing stream of life,
and a perfect contribution.
You will gain
that special vision
it takes to see
perfection
in all the events of your life.

Have you ever seen an imperfect wave?
An imperfect cloud?
An imperfect mountain?
Since these are all perfect,
and easily seen as such,
the next step is easy:
Discover that **every moment** *in time*
is perfect.
And more than just the moment itself,
but also what happens in that moment.
To agree with what happens,
to endorse it
as
"perfect,"
is to be in absolute harmony
with the cause of everything.

If you believe in God,
or any supreme deity,
who is
"causing" things to happen,
then,
by seeing **everything** *that happens*
as
"perfect,"
you have "tuned" yourself,
totally,
to the Supreme Being
whom you believe is causing it.

Once you have harmonized yourself
with the events of your universe
by agreeing with their absolute perfection,
you can then organize future events
more capably,
because you will be
in step
with what already "is."

"Philosophy"
is defined as:
"A theory
of the principals and laws
that regulate the universe,
laws that underlie
all knowledge
and
all reality."
Take a moment to think about that.
***"Laws** that regulate the universe," and*
***"principals** that underlie **all** knowledge and **all** reality."*

It is essential that you live
according to a guiding personal philosophy
that will see you through
the difficult times of
despair, hardship, grief, and despondency
that seem to regularly occur in a person's life -
a philosophy
that gives you
strength,
composure,
patience,
and durability -
a philosophy
that will highlight
your good times
and turn them into exceptional times -
a philosophy
that will change your down feelings
into cheerful feelings
and bring a smile to your face,
a smile that is more
than a brave veneer in the face of adversity,
it is the smile of one who knows
that the mystery of a difficult time
will unravel itself,
revealing
a happy and perfect ending.

A weak philosophy
is a weak way of life.
A strong philosophy,
based on what is true in the universe,
withstands all the rigors and tests of time.

This is your time
to take on the belief
of a powerful,
joy-giving,
happiness-sustaining
philosophy.

Consider for a moment my experience with the fish hook.
What ***could*** *have happened*
as an alternative to what ***did*** *happen?*
Suppose
the instant the fish hook plunged into my finger
I became enraged,
cursed my luck,
grabbed the string,
and tore the hook from my finger,
ripping the flesh!
Suppose this enraged me still further,
and, kicking the rocks and cursing my luck,
it is even possible I could have fallen
and lost my life at that spot.

*Now consider what **did** happen.*
The instant the fish hook pierced my finger,
I acknowledged the event with,
"Perfect!"
After all, the event was over.
It was impossible to back up time
and re-arrange my actions
so that the event would have never take place.
What could I do?
Only one thing.
React to it -
*the **only** option open*
to each of us
*after **every** event -*
the moment of choice.
I could either react
in a way which would bring out
the potential good of the situation,
and, therefore, maintain my superb feelings of the day,
or,
I could curse my luck
and bring out the negative side of the experience.

*Suppose **you** suffered a painful experience*
*that was the **direct cause** of your discovering a truth*
that blessed your life from that time forward.
Would you curse the "accident"
or call it "good fortune?"
***Each** incident in life*
basically
*provides **only** those two choices.*
***Only** with that knowledge*
as a major part of your philosophy,
will you be able to proceed through life
swiftly,
surely,
and successfully.
***Only** with that philosophy*
will you achieve
deep, lasting happiness.
It is that belief alone
that enables you to see the happy side
of seemingly unhappy events,
as well as giving you the insight
to see future events in an optimistic,
knowledgeable way.

Things being "perfect"
is an easy concept to understand.
Consider
what the word "perfect" means.
The dictionary defines it as
"whole" or "complete."

I have added my own definition to the dictionary's:
"That which cannot be added to
or detracted from
in any way which will improve it."
The concept is easy to understand;
however, it is extremely difficult
to put it into use in your everyday life.

First,
it requires you to accept
all that happens
as perfect:
wars,
the splinter in your finger,
earthquakes,
disasters of every kind,
death,
injury,
and loss of possessions,
just to name a few.
Next, it requires you to have
the patience
that goes with your belief in perfection.

Even in the face of
"rotten luck"
you are to be patient,
reacting as though it were
"the best luck possible" -
knowing
that you will soon find out why it was the best luck possible.

Your reward
for following this philosophy
will be your increasing,
conscious *control*
over all situations,
a far more pleasurable "now"
heightened by your vision of a bright and happy future,
together with
your memories of a pleasurable past
that saw you
following your philosophy with sureness.

Those who do not understand that,
who cannot live according to that,
must suffer through the bad times,
fear the future,
and become bitter,
feeling they are victims
who have experienced
rotten luck.

That's not for you.
You are a golden child
of a deathless Universe
where ***everything*** *that happens benefits you.*

Suppose you're feeling really good,
having a fine day,
when someone drives their car over your bicycle!
If you say,
"That's perfect!"
and mean it,
you will be responding to the incident
as though it were a good thing for you.
What happens?
Because the universe is forced to respond
to how you are being at every moment,
you bring out its more pleasant aspects,
its positive potential,
which you then experience.
It's a law of the universe
that ***every action***
produces a result.
If you react to the broken bicycle,
or any event,
as though you are the victim of bad luck,
you will "force" the universe to respond to you
as if it were ***truly*** *bad luck*
and it will produce more unpleasantness
which you then experience.
By keeping in mind
the consequences
of your responses,
you'll experience
happiness-producing results.

Let's play out the broken bike scenario.
You walk over to the driver's side of the car.
The driver is waiting apprehensively for your reaction.
You smile and say,
"That was just right."
You introduce yourself
and the grateful driver offers to pay for the damaged bike.
Your response is,
"That's fine,
I'll accept the payment,
but let's take a moment and see if this event occurred because we needed to meet."
Perhaps the person who ran over the bike
will become your life-long friend.
Suppose, unbeknownst to you,
the bolt that held on your front tire was loose
and the next time you rode it,
you would have had a serious accident going down a steep hill.
Act according to the philosophy
that every event unfolds ***only*** *to benefit you completely*
and you'll ***cause*** *every event*
to continue itself along those lines.

In the beginning,
questions will arise in your mind
that will perhaps weaken your newly awakening belief.
What about the innocent child born with birth defects?
What about disease and sickness?
What about the bombs dropped
on all those innocent people in all those wars?
These and other questions like them
are ones that you will be able to answer for yourself
after you have lived with your philosophy,
when it has seen you through times of despair and pain,
softened the hard times,
and highlighted and brightened even your best days.
In this time of new beginning,
content yourself with seeing perfection in the lost gift,
the disappointing friendship,
the dented fender,
the burned finger,
and the missed bus or plane.
Start with what is easiest
and, one day,
what is hardest
will also be seen
by you
as
"perfect."

The philosophy that you are to keep aware of
through the unfolding of life is:
"I am a perfect being
in a perfect universe
where everything that happens
benefits me
completely."

You *are the doorway*
through which life unfolds.
You *are the mechanism*
by which life is controlled.
When you react to events
in a way that causes you more unpleasantness,
the unpleasantness you experience
will ***appear*** *to confirm*
that what happened
was truly unfortunate.
However,
it was ***your reaction*** *to the event*
which caused the ***continuation*** *of the unpleasantness.*

You're like a railroad switch.
Each time an event occurs
you channel the activity
onto the positive or negative track.
Even though the event hurt you
or took something away from you,
you are still in charge
of channeling it.
You determine its future outcome.

Sometime in your life
something happened to you that seemed awful,
and days, weeks, or even years later, you said,
"That was the best thing
that could have happened to me!"
I write that with certainty
because it has happened to everyone.

Learn to see that perfect truth
now;
condition yourself to see it
at the moment each event occurs.
Know that
"rotten luck"
is a falsehood.

It is hard to believe
that the banged toe,
the torn clothing,
the lost watch,
or the stolen wallet
is completely beneficial for you,
but that is why there are so few
who have their life the way they want it.
Act positively,
and the events coming after will be positive,
and you will then get to enjoy these positive events.
As you progress along this path
you will feel a rising tide of enthusiasm and expectation
welling up within you.
Let it come!

Making It Yours

Exercise Number One.

Turn to the page at the end of this chapter headed "My Philosophy" and write the following:

"I am a perfect being, in a perfect universe, where everything that happens benefits me completely."

Sign your name at the bottom of the page, along with the date.

Exercise Number Two.

You are to spend the rest of today and all of tomorrow viewing the events that you experience as "perfect." You are to call them "perfect," and treat them that way. Believe that they are "just right" happenings and circumstances. The hardest part is keeping aware, remembering what your job is for today and tomorrow. It is so easy to become "caught up" in a situation or an event and forget to see it through the eyes of awareness.

The Boy Scouts have an inner organization called "The Order of the Arrow." During a three day initiation, the chosen candidate must remain silent. He wears a small wooden arrow on a string around his neck. Each time he is caught speaking, a notch is cut into the arrow. At the third speaking offense, the arrow is broken and the candidate is refused admittance to the Order. To help themselves remember to keep silent, most of the candidates hold the arrow between their teeth - especially after they have been caught talking the second time!

Find some memory aid to assist you in keeping aware that you are to see everything that happens today and tomorrow as being totally beneficial to you. Perhaps you can carry a small stone or this book in your hand. If you elect to help yourself remember by carrying a small stone, this book, or some other object, then carry it **all the time**. When it becomes inconvenient or difficult to carry is when it will be most effective in serving as your memory aid. When your mind focuses on whatever you are doing to help yourself remember, replace the focus of your attention with: "All events are perfect and benefit me completely." Avoid tying a string on your finger as a memory aid; most people quickly forget it's there. **Whatever** it takes to keep you aware for today and tomorrow is what you should do. This aspect of seeing things in a good light, a perfect light, is **the heart** of the personal philosophy you are creating for yourself.

Exercise Number Three.

Find a comfortable place and sit quietly for five minutes. Close your eyes and imagine yourself seeing everything that you experience or hear about as perfect events. Imagine yourself switching the negative things you see and hear to the positive track. Do this every day for ten days. Mark your calendar now. Check off a day on your calendar each time you complete a five minute exercise. You may continue this beyond twenty-five days if you wish. This part of the path will train your mind to look for and to find the positive side of events. It will also give you an outlook on life that will delight you day in and day out. You may go on to the next chapter after you have completed one of the five minute sessions and the other exercises in this chapter.

Exercise Number Four.

Enjoy another half hour of pleasure. Begin by saying, "I, (your name), give myself permission to enjoy a half hour of pleasure." Fulfill this exercise indoors. Remember, if it turns out to be less than pleasurable, start over or choose another pleasure exercise. When you've completed this exercise, write a brief summary on the page headed "Pleasure Exercise Number Three."

Complete these exercises before going on to Chapter Four.

"My Philosophy"

Signature Date

"Pleasure Exercise Number Three"

____

Date Completed

Chapter Four

You Are The Center

Some astronomers say
that our Universe
has an exact center.
They also say
that it is most unlikely that planet Earth
is ***at*** *that center.*

However,
the Universe
and the center
we are concerned with
is that of
your "personal" Universe.

Your Personal Universe exists
only
because you do.
It is the Universe
that ***you*** *perceive*
with ***your*** *senses.*
If you were absent from your personal Universe,
your personal Universe would be absent as well.
In that Universe,
you ***are*** *the center.*

__Being__ the center,
is more than being __at__ the center.
If you were only at the center,
when you moved,
you would move away from the center.
__Being__ the center
means that the center moves as you do.

The Universe is changing
and evolving
as a result of forces outside of you;
a continual moment-by-moment creation.
But to some extent,
you participate in that continuing creation.

Suppose you live on a farm where there is a stream, and you widen it and deepen it so it becomes a pond. You put in some frogs and some Lilly pads, and you plant a tree on its edge whose branches hang over and trail in the water. Birds build their nests in the tree, wild ducks come and land on the pond, and wild animals come to drink. On its own, the grass grows, the fish and frogs multiply, and nature fulfills herself. As you can see, by building the pond, you have participated in the continuing creation of the world around you.

Suppose you were a teacher and the children whose lives you influenced became, doctors, farmers, biologists, scientists, presidents, astronauts, engineers, carpenters, and other occupations of their choosing. From that point forward, both the children and the Universe would be forever different because you existed.

It is only when you are
***fully** aware*
that you are the center
of your personal Universe,
creating
*and influencing **everything** around you*
that you will understand
how important
is your every act.

Take a moment to imagine
yourself
as the center of your personal Universe.
Imagine that everything you say and do and think
affects everyone and everything
within your personal Universe.
Put the book down
*and do that **now** for at least one minute.*

Holding that image in your mind
will cause
you to take care
with your every action,
with your every thought,
and with everything you say.

What every incident
in my life,
in your life
comes down to is this:
I am the center of my Universe,
you are the center of your Universe.
I determine what happens for me,
you determine what happens for you.

Up to this point in your life,
you've created many of the events in your life,
some times knowingly,
sometimes not.
Sometimes you've created pain and hardship
for yourself
without knowing it was
you
who were the cause.

Events are being created around you
by outside forces,
but even so,
the power to
assist
in the creation of those events
exists
within
you.

As you learned in an earlier chapter,
***your reaction** to those events,*
determines
the outcome of those events.
*You are **always** using your power*
to create and influence events.

You're like a radio station that transmits
constantly.
***Whatever** you broadcast*
goes out over the airwaves
in every direction,
affecting everything around you.
If you're broadcasting fear,
fear is projected
to everything around you
and brings those things
to you
that are attracted by fear.

If you're broadcasting
power and confidence,
everyone and everything around you
is affected
positively.

A man in the mid-west owned a financially successful sandwich shop. There were nearly always people in line to buy his products. He gave away free pickles, free potato chips, sometimes a free soft drink or cup of coffee, and he put generous portions in all of his sandwiches; the sandwiches bulged with food. One day, his son, a Chicago stock broker, whom he hadn't seen in several years, came to visit. After a few days spent observing his father's shop, the son told his father that in his opinion, he was making a big mistake giving away all the free items and in putting such generous amounts in his sandwiches. "The country's economy is in bad shape," the son said. "People are out of work and there is less money to spend. Unless you cut back on the free items and the generous portions, you too, will soon find yourself in a bad way."

The son left and went home to his distant city. The father followed his son's advice. He stopped giving away the free items and he cut down on the generous portions of food he put in his sandwiches. Soon afterwards, when many of his disappointed customers had stopped coming, he wrote to his son and said, "You're right, son! The country's economy **is** in bad shape, and I'm experiencing the results of it right here in my sandwich shop!"

The poor economy
the son saw all around him
was real.
However,
in the midst of the poor economy,
his father was running
a very successful sandwich shop.
His father was
unaware
that times were hard,
that many people were out of work,
and that money was scarce.
When he heard about it from his son,
he began to
***act as if it were so**,*
*and brought about the **only** possible result:*
a negative, fearful, ungenerous experience of life;
an experience he believed to be
"out there."
Was it "out there?"
Who cut back on the portions of food?
Who eliminated the "give away" items?
Who was it that made the first move?
You know the answer.

Can you now answer
for the areas in your own life
that you are dissatisfied with?
It's harder to see in your own life
because you've been thinking
for so long
that the reason the way things are is
"out there."
What's really happening is that what's
"out there,"
is reacting
to
you.

Making It Yours

Exercise Number One

Memorize the statement, "I am the center of my personal Universe." Write it down, carry it about, put it where you'll be sure to see it often. Allow this truth to live in your mind. A major purpose of this path is to increase your awareness that you are the center of your personal Universe, that you influence everyone and everything you come in contact with. It is designed to keep you more aware for more minutes out of every day that you are affecting everyone and everything around you by being, "who you are."

Exercise Number Two

Pretend to have the responsibility for actually causing every event that occurs in your life. You will have to stretch your imagination for this, but you are to include rain, sunshine, automobile accidents, blooming flowers, a stubbed toe, and even such trivia as a torn cuticle. What you are to do is to take full and complete responsibility for every single act of creation you are aware of. If you wake up in the morning and it's a foggy day, look out the window and say, "I have ordered this wonder, foggy morning." Act "as if" you were responsible for the mist you now behold, and deal with it as if you had ordered **the most beneficial weather possible for yourself.** Make believe that it is exactly suited to your particular needs of that day.

For example, the next time you plan a Sunday picnic and you wake up and its raining, you have your work cut out for you. Make believe that you caused it to rain, and that it is for your best benefit. You may discover later that the area you had chosen for your picnic was the scene of a riot that day, or that because you stayed home an important event took place that caused you to bless that rainy morning that caused you to change your plans. After you have enough "rainy day experiences" that turn out perfectly, you'll quickly get the knack of it. One of the best benefits is keeping yourself feeling good about the ever-unfolding events around you.

In the course of your lifetime, you may never experience being the actual cause of a rainfall or a foggy morning—that's OK. What's important is the practice of taking responsibility for the rainy day or foggy morning, treating it as though you were the cause, and that you caused it as the best event possible. That'' important: "The **best** event **possible**." It's practice. And, like everything else, the more you do it, the better you become at doing it. If a person greets you cheerfully, take it upon yourself to believe you have caused it. If a person greets you crossly, or treats you with less respect, consideration or love than you would like them to , take responsibility for that by saying to yourself: "I created this. It's for my best benefit. I can change the way this person is responding to me by making a change in myself."

Once you have decided what the change should be, make it. It may take you awhile to know what inner changes will bring about the desired results, but with practice, you'll soon find out.

Taking responsibility for all that happens to you is hard. In the first place, it takes a big stretch of your imagination. But the hardest part, by far, is giving up acting the part of a powerless person. That involves giving up the self-defeating comfort of being able to blame factors other than yourself for seeming failures. The reward for your being successful in this undertaking will be the equivalent of having driven a car backwards all your life, and then having someone show you that certain gears make it go forward—and fast!

Exercise Number Three

At the end of this chapter is page headed, "My Hopes." On that page write down what you hope for yourself. Search your mind, let your imagination roam. Think about what you truly want for yourself. Then, regardless of how difficult or far-fetched what you want seems, write it down. Be as descriptive as you can in writing what your hopes are. If, for instance, you want to take a trip around the world, describe it in as much detail as possible. If you hope for a mate or a friend, describe what the person will be like. If you hope for a possession of some kind, describe it in as much detail as you can.

In deciding what your hopes are, keep them personal. One reader's first two hopes were: "I hope my son is financially successful," and "I hope my son finds happiness." Neither one of those hopes is what is intended here. Your hopes are to be for yourself alone, although they might include someone else, such as hoping to find a mate or a friend. As you progress on this path, you may find that your hopes change. If that happens, change your "hopes list." You may add to your list or cross out hopes you lose the desire for. When a hope is fulfilled, simply write "fulfilled" next to it. If you run out of room to write, cut a piece of paper to the size of the pages in this book, and write neatly across the top of the page, "My Hopes." Place it in the book next to the "Hopes" page. Keep all your pages. You may list any number of hopes you want, many or only a few. Then sign your name on the line provided. Give this exercise plenty of thought because one of the most important steps in bringing about what you want for yourself is to first imagine it. Review your hopes list **every time** you begin a new chapter.

Exercise Number Four

Enjoy another half hour of pleasure. Begin by saying, "I (your name), give myself permission to enjoy another half hour of pleasure. Fulfill this exercise by yourself. You may fulfill it where there are other people about, but do not take anyone with you or arrange to meet anyone. If you meet someone seemingly "by chance," that's fine. Remember, at the end of your half hour, if it was less than pleasurable, start over then or later, or choose another pleasure exercise. After you have completed this exercise, write a brief summary on the page headed, "Pleasure Exercise Number Four."

Complete these exercise before going on to Chapter Five.

My Hopes

Signature Date

“Pleasure Exercise Number Four”

____

Date completed

Chapter Five

Your Personal Universe

(Review your hopes list,
read slowly.)

How far can you see?
Put the book down for a moment
and answer the question for yourself.
Do that ***now****.*

I have heard many answers.
Some people say,
"Whatever the distance is to the furthest object,"
or, "As far as the skyline."
Others say,
"It depends on the day."
Still others say they can see the sun,
which is 93 million miles away,
or they can see the stars,
which are hundreds of millions of light years away.

Actually,
the ***only*** *thing you can see are light rays*
as they enter your eyes
after being radiated or reflected from an object.
Your eyes are ***receivers****.*

Inside of each eye
are about one hundred million rods and cones.
These rods and cones are stimulated
by the rays of light that enter your eye
which, in turn,
create impulses
that travel along the optic nerve system to the brain.
The brain receives those impulses
and forms a picture.
Where do you think the picture is?
Is it "out there"
in front of your eyes,
as it appears to be?
The picture is ***totally*** *inside of your head -*
formed ***by*** *your brain,*
within *your brain.*
Stop reading a moment and picture that.

Think about what the explanation of
this picture-making process means to you.
Think about how it changes
your relationship to the "outside" world.
Do you realize that, in your lifetime,
you have never actually seen an object?
The ***only*** *thing you ever saw were light rays*
being radiated by or reflected from objects.
Every rock, every tree, every person,
every house, every car,
everything *you have ever seen,*
or thought you saw,
including yourself,
was just a picture formed inside your head
when light rays bounced off the objects
and entered your eyes.
The view you have of the world
is simply a picture
that ***appears*** *to be outside,*
but actually
is inside your head.

Are the images you see
the same images that everyone else sees?
Have you ever seen two faces ***exactly*** *alike?*
Two noses, two eyes, two ears?
Since these are ***all*** *different,*
can you imagine that the hundred million
rods and cones in your eyes
are different from the hundred million
rods and cones that are in every other person's eyes?
Even if only a few of the rods and cones were different,
you would still form pictures
that were slightly different
from those of everyone else.

There's also a difference beyond
the mechanical process of seeing.
When individuals form these inner pictures,
they react to those pictures
based upon their past experiences.
One woman sees the color red
and thinks of a beautiful rose
given to her a long time ago,
reminding her of a great love.
Another woman sees the same shade of red
and remembers the matador's cape
and how shocked and horrified she was
when the bull was killed.
They react to the color in different ways.

Suppose there were ten people
sitting in a circle
around a small pond
with the moon nearly overhead.
Suppose all ten pointed to the reflection
they saw of the moon on the pond.
Every person would point to a different place
according to where they were sitting -
and yet they would think
that they were all looking at the same reflection.

The human equipment with which you hear
is also slightly different
from the human equipment
with which everyone else hears.
Similarly, your senses of touch, taste,
and smell are different from everyone else's.
Everything
is different
for every person.
The difference may be only slight,
but it's that **slight** *difference*
that makes **all** *the difference.*

One day, when I was talking to a small group of people, I picked up a toy figure of the Pink Panther made of some plastic material that could be formed into different positions and I put it into a standing position with its arms upraised. I then asked the twelve people in the room what they thought the Pink Panther was doing. One said he was praying, one said he was stretching, one said he was dancing, and another said he was singing. Each person saw the Pink Panther doing something different. One person had even seen him holding a rock and the rock was only imagined!

*It is like that with **all** events in life.*
Each person sees them differently,
reacts to them differently,
and causes different results to occur.
One sees an event as a loss,
another sees the same event as a gain.

Now, what does all this mean to you?
*It means that **everything** you*
see,
hear,
touch,
smell,
taste,
or experience in any way
is different for you
*than it is for **everyone** else.*
It means that to be able to proceed
correctly and successfully
you have to rely solely and completely
*on **what's true for you**.*
If you rely on what's true for another,
you'll probably be slightly off course.

In one of the workshops I gave there was a seventeen-year-old boy named Alex. From the beginning, he readily absorbed the workshop information and made it part of himself. One evening, after we had thoroughly covered the topic of having things the way we wanted them, Alex called his best friend, Tex, and asked him if he'd like to go to the movies.

"Sure," Tex replied, "what do you want to see?"

"Let's go see the new movie at the Palace Theater."

"Well, O.K." Tex said hesitantly, "but it's opening night, and we may not get in."

Alex was fresh from the workshop, the concepts vividly in his mind, and he eagerly responded, "**I'm** going to see the eight o'clock show **tonight**, with you! I'll pick you up in twenty minutes."

Alex was feeling a little excited and the phrase was going through his mind, "I **can** have things the way I want them, oh boy!"

When they arrived at the movie theater they were greeted with a sign in the ticket window that read "SOLD OUT." It was five minutes to eight.

"They're sold out," Tex said disappointedly, "but if we hurry we can still get to see something else."

"Come on," Alex replied, "we're here to see **this** movie."

He walked to the ticket window and asked for two tickets to the eight o'clock show. The girl at the window said the show was completely sold out, but she would sell them tickets to the ten o'clock show. Tex again asked Alex to leave.

"Come on," he said, "If we hurry, we can still get to see another movie."

"This is opening night," Alex replied, "and I came to see **this** show."

Alex found the manager of the theater and explained to him what he wanted. The manager said he was sorry, but the computer sold exactly as many tickets as there were seats in the theater and that there simply were no more tickets. It was now eight o'clock. Alex found the owner of the theater, who was smiling happily because it was opening night and hundreds of people had squeezed into his theater. Alex explained their situation.

"We know that you're sold out for this performance, but surely there are two seats somewhere in your big theater."

The tuxedoed owner told them about the computer and all the tickets being sold and that even if he did let them in they wouldn't be able to sit together. Alex knew that everything would be the way he wanted it, if only he believed it and acted out of his belief.

"That's all right, we can sit separately," he said.

The owner looked a little doubtful but said, "O.K. boys, go on in."

"How much do we owe you?" asked Alex.

"Forget it," said the owner. "This one's on me."

They each shook his hand as they raced inside the theater and found two seats together in the center section about ten rows back from the screen - just in time to see the beginning of the movie.

"This is great!" whispered Tex.

"It sure is!" replied his best friend.

Tex meant, "It's great we got in to see the movie."

Alex meant, "It's great that I can have things the way I want them!"

That was only a movie.
That was only two friends
doing a little something extra
to get to see a show.
But,
Alex used a universal principle
and used it perfectly.
That night it was only a movie,
another time he will use the same principle,
perhaps to purchase the house
everyone says is not for sale,
or to invent a new machine
everyone says cannot be invented.
That attitude,
that "inner knowing,"
when fully developed,
will be
"what's true for Alex,"
and it will carry him
to the fulfillment
of his dreams and
a wonderfully satisfying life,
having things the way he wants them.

In every situation
there are generally two
basic options open to you.
Tex's attitude
when they first got to the theater,
demonstrates exactly where one of those
options will lead -
directly to failure.
He said,
"We'll never get to see this movie,
but if we hurry we can see something else."
He was hurrying to failure.
Alex's response,
"We're here to see **this** *movie,"*
leads directly to success.

This is much more than a simple situation
with an unusual theater owner.
This is a universal principal in action.
Alex actually created the result!
Spend a moment to fully understand this.
Alex created his future in a special way.
All the pieces of reality were there for both boys:
the theater,
five minutes until show time,
the "SOLD OUT" sign,
the ticket seller,
the manager,
the owner.
Tex saw them differently
from the way Alex saw them
and used them according to the way
he usually used his pieces of reality -
he was ready and very willing
to accept less than he wanted.
Alex, with his new workshop information,
created a success that reinforced his belief
that he can have things just the way he wants them!
Now it's your turn...

Here's the heart of that concept:
You actually participate,
moment by moment,
in the creation of
your universe.

It's an easy concept to understand,
but a difficult one to keep aware of
and to use in your everyday life.
When you believe
you can do something,
you ***actually create***
the stream of events
that brings about
what you believe*.*
Those things you fail to believe you can do,
you fail to bring about.

I was waiting at a small airport recently when I struck up a conversation with one of the airport workers, a young man of about twenty. During our talk he found out I had a private pilot's license and he said that he, too, would love to get his pilot's license. I asked him why he was waiting.

"Too much money," he said. "As soon as I found out how much the lessons cost, I gave up the idea,"

"There's opportunity all around you!" I responded energetically. "You work at an airport! Talk to the owners of the planes, talk to the pilots, talk to the crew members, find out if there's something you can do in exchange for lessons. When **you** decide you can't do it, it's over! You can just as easily decide to do it and in time you'll have your pilot's license!"

He shrugged his shoulders, looked at me as if I were a little strange, and said, "Nope, I don't think so, it's too expensive. When I heard how much it cost I just turned away from it."

"But you're turning away from life, from yourself, from opportunity, and you're acting as if you're powerless! Are you powerless?"

He shrugged his shoulders, laughed a little, looked at me again as if I were strange, and walked away.

There are always two obvious choices
in every situation.
You can either take positive action
to bring about what you want,
or you can shrug your shoulders and walk away.
Your success and failure is brought about
by what you believe.
For a limitation to be valid
you must accept it.
Start believing
that you are a special person
who has the ability
to do what you want to do.
***Act** on that belief!*

It is a difficult task -
to break out of a shell
of restricted thinking
and into your perfect personal universe
of expanded thinking,
*but you **can** do it!*
Until recently,
you've lived your life believing
that having what you want is limited,
so your actions were based on that belief,
and, consequently, you produced results
consistent with your belief.
Your beliefs were then reinforced by "reality."
Now ask yourself: " Who created the reality?"

It is important that you
fully understand what it means to
"produce results based upon your belief."
If you believe you **can** *do something,*
you will act
based on your belief.
If you believe something is impossible to do,
you will fail to even begin.
Both results
will convince you
of the "rightness" of your actions,
or the lack of them.

Read the next paragraph aloud, as though you had written it.

"**This** is **my** time to have the circumstances of **my** life the way **I** want them. "All That Is" reacts to **me**. In the midst of the always unfolding, universal events, **I** participate in directing and controlling how things are in my personal universe. **I** participate in creating the circumstances of my life, moment by moment. To change those outward circumstances I make changes in myself. **I** affect "All That Is" by being "Who I Am" at every moment. I **am** a pure, bright spirit - **a perfect being**. I act with that knowledge and the Universe responds in the only way possible - with what I want."

You can already feel new awareness
and capability within you,
but perhaps you're still uncertain
how far it extends.
It extends to the height, width, and depth
of your personal universe.
In that universe,
its most basic, most important law
is
"cause and effect."
***You** are the cause,*
*and **you** produce the effects*
by being who you are at every moment.

In one of my workshops there was a young man, Harvey. who had gone to discos for many years to watch people dance. He yearned to dance with the women, but he could only stand on the side-lines, watching, because the thought of walking across the dance floor and asking one of them to dance was too frightening. The image of being rejected and then having to make that long, embarrassing walk back again, with everyone knowing what had happened, was more than he could handle. He just couldn't bring himself to do it. So the years passed and his longing grew.

If you could have seen Harvey and heard his sad tale, you would have chuckled as I did, for he was a fine looking young man about six feet tall, with broad shoulders, a fair complexion, and smooth, even features. It seemed as if any woman would be pleased to dance with him.

One Friday evening, after he had been in the workshop about two weeks, Harvey went to his favorite disco and took up his accustomed place against the wall. Suddenly, he remembered that he was in a workshop and had learned that this was a perfect workout situation, and the outcome, whatever it was, would be a complete benefit to him. He brought his perfect image to mind, walked across the dance floor to the woman to whom he was most attracted, and invited her to dance. She was delighted! That night Harvey danced with all the women of his choice. He was elated! The following Monday evening at the workshop, he was so proud of himself and so filled with happiness and certainty, that he told us that he believed he could do anything! He talked about his new plans, his new ideas, and told us that he was surely able to fulfill all of them.

The capability and the strength
to do all of that
had **always** *been within Harvey;*
he only had to call upon it.

It's the very same capability
that is within you,
waiting for your call.

One of the greatest truths available,
at this or any moment in time,
is that you are
the master maker and molder
of your personal universe;
as you believe,
so it is for you.

Is there anything that you want?
Are there any changes you'd like to make?
***Now** is the time.*

Because
"Now"
*is **a continually unfolding event**,*
all you can do
at this instant
is to make the decision
to bring about
what you want.
But
your decision will live within you,
continually influencing your actions,
*and it **will** eventually bring you*
to the achievement of your goals.
*It's your **ever-present** willpower,*
directed toward a precise outcome,
that will lead you
successfully
to your goal.

Give in to your wholesome desires!
***Allow** yourself to be drawn*
toward your goals.
Believe that you will arrive at those goals
safely and happily.
As you travel,
remember that the universal law
of cause and effect is absolute -
if you put out good positive vibrations,
that is what you shall experience.
For acting knowledgeably,
treating each incident as
"just right,"
everything in your personal universe
will reflect your positive actions.
Pause a moment;
think what it means
to have
your entire personal universe
reflect your actions!
Treat yourself well by being
the best person you know how to be.
You can dance if you want to!

Making It Yours

Exercise Number One.

Find a place where you can sit comfortably and quietly, free from interruption. Close your eyes and mentally go back to your childhood and then come forward by separating your life into "blocks of time." For instance: pre-school, early school, summer vacations, trips, moving from one home to another, different ages, memorable events, different jobs. As you remember your way forward from childhood, remember those events that seemed hurtful to you because of things that were done to you by others. It can be any kind of hurt - physical, financial, moral, or emotional.

Review each incident in as much detail as you can, then carefully switch it onto a positive track. See it as beneficial in every way. Think of events which have occurred since the time of the hurtful event that were extra nice and hook those events together with the previous hurtful event. Realize that the later events were part of a "sequence" of which the hurtful event was a part. Use the good events as "leverage" to help put the hurtful event onto the positive track. Even though in the beginning you see it as hurtful, call it beneficial. Say it's good without believing it if you need to. Stay with it until the hurt is gone and you've freed yourself from the burden of carrying a "hurt" from your past. Just as it's nice to live in a clean home, wear clean clothes, and be clean yourself, it's nice to have a clean past - it provides you with a happy "now" and expectations for a bright future. Stay with it until it's done. **It would almost be better for you to remain seated forever than to get up carrying around all that extra baggage from the past.** It clutters up "now." You have far too much to do in your future to permit your past to slow you down. Besides, you and the Universe have moved on. Don't permit yourself to stay back there, rooted in time, at place where you received your hurt. Take a deep breath, smile, and move on. **You're doing it for yourself.** It is necessary to do that to achieve happiness. It takes our full awareness just to stay in step with the ever-unfolding Universe. There is no time to remain in the past, or carry its hurts into the future. **Free yourself.**

All that happens -
now,
then,
sooner,
later -
happens for your greatest benefit.

Allow that knowledge to live in your consciousness
and
you will always live
in
"The World of Perfect,"
handling new events
in a way that leaves you whole,
in charge,
feeling good,
and grateful for the occurrences of the day.

Accomplish that exercise in two sessions of a half hour each. There should be at least a two hour period between the two sessions. A half hour is the least amount of time you should spend in each session. You may have as many sessions as you need in order to accomplish your exercise, but for the purpose of going on to the next chapter you may consider this exercise completed after accomplishing two half hour sessions.

Exercise Number Two.

Give yourself permission to create and experience a half hour of pleasure. Begin by saying, "I, (your name), give myself permission to experience a half hour of pleasure." Before selecting your new pleasure exercise, read each of your summaries for the previous pleasure exercises. This time, push your boundaries out a bit more so you can experience more of the pleasure life has to offer. Fulfill this exercise with another person. Tell the person it's an exercise in a path you're following. If the exercise turns out to be less than pleasurable, start over or choose another exercise or another person. After the exercise is completed write a brief summary on the page headed "Pleasure Exercise Number Five."

Complete these exercises before going on to Chapter Six.

"Pleasure Exercise Number Five"

____
Date Completed

Chapter Six

Possibilities

By now,
you have seen the universe respond
to your new way of being,
which has increased your confidence
in yourself.
It is now time
to shake off
still more of the beliefs you've accepted
that are preventing you
from having what you want.

Deep in your innermost mental recesses
should live the belief:
"All things are possible
for those who believe
that all things are possible."
This truth
is a precious jewel
in your treasure chest of knowledge;
you've got to know in your heart -
"I can do it".
Do what?
Anything!

One evening, as I started a workshop, I asked everyone in the room what they would most like to do if they had all the power they wanted.

In reply to this question, a tall, handsome, rugged looking iron worker named Patrick looked at me and said, “If I had all the power I wanted, I’d want to work on the bridge.” He sure looked as if he could do anything. He was about six and half feet tall, wore cowboy boots, a belt with a big, silver buckle, and he looked really strong.

“The bridge?” I asked. “What bridge?”

He replied indignantly, “What do you mean, **what** bridge? There’s only **one** bridge - Golden Gate!”

“The Golden Gate bridge is in San Francisco. If you want to work on that bridge, what are you doing in Los Angeles?”

“It’s not that easy,” he said forcefully. “You can’t just go work on `The Bridge’!”

“Why not?”

“Are you kidding?” he replied in an unbelieving tone. “You can’t just go work on “The Bridge!” First you’ve got to win your suspenders and your hard hat. They only take **the best** up there!”

“What do you mean, you’ve got to win your suspenders and your hard hat? Don’t you have those things?”

He looked at me as if I really didn’t know anything at all and replied, “Those are levels of iron working, grades of expertise. It’s more than that though, even when you’ve reached those levels, you’ve got to **know** somebody. That bridge is run by a union, a tough union!" And he added reverently, "It's the Iron Workers' Union."

"Oh, so does that mean that you can't work on the bridge?"

"Of course that's what it means!"

After a long pause I asked, "Can you see that **your belief** in the way things are is what prevents you from going to San Francisco and getting a job on the bridge?"

"It's not **my belief** that keeps me from going to San Francisco; it's **the Union!**"

"Oh, **the Union**! What would you say if I told you I could go to San Francisco and get a job working on the bridge and I'm not even a union member - or an iron worker?"

He laughed uproariously at that and began to ridicule me, saying, "You? They wouldn't let you within a mile of that bridge! Do you know how dangerous that work is? Do you think they're going to risk their jobs and all that liability by allowing you to work on the bridge? You must be crazy! Huh! That's the stupidest thing I've ever heard!"

"Patrick, suppose I went to the person in charge of hiring for the Golden Gate bridge, and told them I was writing a book about the greatest bridge in the world and the men who work on it, and that to gather information, I wanted to work on the bridge for a day. What do you think they'd say?"

"What do I **think** they'd say? I **know** what they'd say. They'd get you away from that bridge quicker than you could bat an eyelash! You don't know how **dangerous** that work is! They would **never** let you work on the bridge."

"Well, Patrick, what if I went to the foreman of the bridge and told him that one of his fellow iron workers, a man named Patrick, had given up his will to live as a great human being, a great iron worker. Suppose I told him that Patrick no longer believed in himself, but he had one great desire and that was to work on the greatest bridge in America, the Golden Gate. Suppose I told the foreman that Patrick had lost so much confidence in himself that he despaired of **ever** being able to reach that goal. Suppose I told him that if I could get to work on the bridge, even for **one** day, it might inspire Patrick enough, and give him enough courage, to continue on as the truly great man and iron worker he really is! Now, Patrick, what do you think he'd say to that?"

Patrick threw back his head and laughed. "I think that is the biggest load of garbage I've ever heard!"

"O.K., Patrick, because you believe you have to win your suspenders and your hard hat and know somebody in the Union in order to get to work on the bridge, you have to remain here in Los Angeles, **rooted** here by your belief. If I **believe** what you tell me, that it's impossible for me to get a job on the bridge, I also have to remain here in Los Angeles without ever going to San Francisco to even **attempt** to work on the bridge. On the other hand, if I believe all things are possible for those who believe that all things are possible, I can go to San Francisco and, one way or another, I'll get to work on the bridge."

"Look," he said, "I'm getting kind of mad. I don't want to hear any more of this!"

He quit the workshop at the end of the first week.

In the 1920's, an engineer from Chicago named Joseph Strauss stood at the mouth of the San Francisco Bay, which is called "Golden Gate," and said, **"I can build a bridge across the entrance to this bay!"**

Engineers said it was impossible. The press ridiculed the project. Geologists laughed and said that the first earthquake would quickly demolish any bridge across San Francisco's Golden Gate.

For nearly five years, Joseph Strauss and his builders fought tides, public opinion, wind, storms, and the ocean itself until they finished what is today one of the most beautiful landmarks in the world. It took a year to build the south tower, which is as high as a ten-story building and it had to be built underwater! The bridge still stands, a monument to the courage, the determination, and the belief of Joseph Strauss.

On one hand,
we have Joseph Strauss,
the man who engineered
and supervised the building of
the Golden Gate Bridge.
On the other hand,
we have Patrick, our iron worker,
whose belief system prevented him
from getting a job on that wonderful bridge.
More than that,
it even prevented him
from going to San Francisco
to ***attempt*** *to get a job on the bridge.*
Do you know the difference
between these two men?

One believed he could -
the other believed he couldn't!

One man had the courage
and the belief
that he could design and build a bridge across San Francisco's Golden Gate.
The other man,
***after this incredible feat was accomplished**,*
could not even to go to San Francisco
to apply for a job on that same bridge!
*What a **vast** difference between these two men*
and yet they are separated from each other
only by what they believed!

At one point during the filming of a movie I directed, I was in Tallahassee, Florida, at a farm where there lived five "caretakers" - five really nice people who were allowed to live there in exchange for looking after the property. The head of the little farm group, Don, was married to a lovely girl, Sandy, and they had a newborn son, Seth. The thirty-five of us who made up the cast and crew arrived there with our buses, trucks, cars, and expensive equipment, and even though I barely had enough money to sustain us, it looked as if we must be wealthy. In contrast, the five on the farm were having a difficult time getting through the winter because even though it was Florida, it was northern Florida where the winters are mighty chilly.

One evening, shortly after we arrived, Don showed me around the little farm house and at one point he looked at me and his eyes flashed as he pointed to a Bible on the mantle.

"You see that book?" he said, "that's the **only** book I've read in the last ten years!"

He talked awhile about how wonderful a book it was. He was very powerful in his conviction that his Bible contained all the information and all the guidance he needed and he was very proud of his dedication to it. He stated that he lived his life by it.

A week later, at the end of our filming there, Don invited me to stay and have a final dinner with "the family." It was a warm, friendly gathering.

After dinner Don said wishfully, "If only we could get to Hawaii - I have friends there. You know, in Hawaii my wife and baby and I could stay on the beach! The weather is just perfect. We could live in a tent and eat avocados and mangoes and grapefruit right off the trees! We could live off the land!" He gave a long sigh and shook his head sadly. "It would be marvelous if only I could get us there."

I asked him why he remained in Florida.

"Ahh, you know, we, ah, we don't have any money," he said with a bit of embarrassment.

"Do you need money to get to Hawaii?" I inquired.

"Well, how do you get there?" he asked.

"You get your baby and your wife, you pack up the things you want and you walk out the door," I answered in a matter of fact way. "You figure out were Hawaii is, and head for it."

"Oh, I know the route and all that, you go to California first but this is February. What happens if we get to the middle of Texas and run into a snowstorm and we don't get picked up? We have four-month-old Seth; what do we do then?"

"Good, Don, that's really good. What happens if you go out there, stick your thumb out, and the first person that comes by, picks you up and takes you all the way to California?"

"That's a mighty big "if," he said.

"Yeah, but your "if" keeps you here. My "if" gets you to California!"

"I don't know, I hear what you're saying, but I don't think I can take that risk."

"Don, you have very little money and your circumstances here on the farm are very poor. So, I suggest you put your Bible to some good use. Tear the pages out of it and use them to start your fires."

"What! Burn my Bible! Are you crazy? That's the word of God! You lookin' for trouble?"

"Come on Don, if you believed what you read in your Bible, you would go out on the road and put your thumb out and end up on the other side of the country. **That's how a powerful person who has faith acts.** Some people believe in God, some in themselves, some in luck. But the people who are powerful and believe in **something**, **act** on their belief!"

Don was still angry because I had said he had little faith and should burn his Bible, so I said, "I'll tell you what Don, I'll give you a place to go in Los Angeles, if you ever get enough courage or belief to go."

I wrote down the name and address of a friend who lived in California and said, "Somebody is almost always at the house who will welcome you."

I shook hands with everyone and left.

I returned the next morning to say a final good-bye, but Don, Sandy, and Seth were gone! Four days later I got a call from my friend in Los Angeles who said "Don, Sandy, and Seth are here!" They stayed with my friend in California about six weeks while Don worked as a carpenter and then they made their way to Hawaii where they "lived off the land" for the winter.

When you wish to do something,
anything,
believe that you have the capability
to do it.
In the beginning,
you may have to pretend that it's true.
However,
make your plan
and follow it through confidently.
Allow yourself to act
with the power that is already within you.
It is a perfect and completely capable force
which is yours to use,
as you wish,
in every situation.

I heard a man in his eighties
being interviewed one day
and he said,
"I only regret the things I didn't do."
How true!
This is a life for doing!
This is a life for getting on with it!
The only two elements that you ever need
to bring about what you want
are your belief that it is possible
and the will to do it.

Beware of your old conditioning!
In earlier years you learned
that many goals were closed to you.
You learned that many opportunities
were outside of your capabilities.
Change those beliefs now!
Look at all goals as being achievable.
Know that you can achieve
what you wish to achieve,
that you can have
what you want to have.
Let your imagination roam freely,
looking into the wonderful world
of total possibility that surrounds you,
knowing that your choices are limited
***only** when **you** accept the limitations.*

Was there ever a time in your life
when an opportunity came along
and you failed to take it?
Did you ever have the desire to do something
"bigger than life"?
Is it something you still want to do?
Now
is your time to do it!

Making It Yours

Exercise Number One.

Have a talk with someone about the possibility that "All things are possible for those who believe that all things are possible." Spend fifteen minutes having this conversation. Inform your conversation partner that you want to have this discussion as an exercise in a path you're following. The outcome of the discussion is of little importance. What is of major importance is that you are opening your mind to the possibility that you can have what you want. It's a means of stretching your mind. Stay away from "prove-it" topics like physically floating in air or mentally moving heavy objects, they will only reinforce the limiting perceptions you now believe in. Instead, discuss the possibility of having everything you currently want. Take the position that you can have it, just the way you want it. If the person to whom you're talking disagrees, which is very likely, that's perfect. You have all the answers inside yourself and this will help you pull them out so you can hear them.

In my workshops there frequently were people who would argue fiercely with me about some concept or another, and in my effort to bring forth my best response, I would hear myself saying something for the first time, something new that increased my understanding.

The person who takes the other side of this discussion is arguing for his or her limitations. If this person argues well enough and long enough, he or she will get to own those limitations.

By taking the position in your discussion that all things are possible, you have aligned yourself on the side where you must be if you are to have what you want. As you make progress on this path you will become ever more capable of setting forth reasons and arguments for your position. After a while, the reasons will be discarded because you'll be a living demonstration of the truth of your beliefs. Actually, you are now a living demonstration of your beliefs. So stretch your mind to accept entirely that you are capable of accomplishing your goals and desires.

Exercise Number Two.

Sit quietly for ten minutes where you will be free from interruption and think if there is a belief left anywhere in your mind that there is something you will fail at, even if you totally set yourself to accomplish it. If you think of something, carefully remove the limitations from your thinking. Expand your belief system to include being fully capable of accomplishing whatever you want. The way to do that is to think of what you want and then say to yourself, "I can do it." At first you may have to pretend it's true but there is a part inside of you that hears you say, "I can do it," and responds to it.

Beginning to do something, even though you are having a hard time seeing **how** you will be able to **finish** it, is one of the major steps in accomplishing your heart's desires. It's like seeing a mountain in the distance that you have to cross in order to get to a place that holds a great treasure. From where you are, it looks as though it's impossible to climb the distant mountain, but you have an inner belief you can do it and the way to start is to take the first step toward the mountain. **Take that step believing you will arrive at your goal**. As you get closer and closer, you will finally see the small trail that leads up and over the top - the one that was hidden to you until your courage and belief brought you close enough to see it.

And I will tell you of a great treasure;
the trail is ***always*** *there!*

It's that inner belief that brings you to every goal. **The real treasure though, is in the traveling**. **That's** where life reveals itself in its moment by moment unfolding. As it unfolds, let it find you traveling along, saying with a smile, "Here I am, traveling this wonder filled path, believing all will be well!" And, of course, "All That Is" responds in the only way it can - by fulfilling your belief.

Exercise Number Three.

Sit quietly for a half hour and remember, beginning with your childhood, the times when you failed at something - failed to start, failed to finish, failed to do. As you remember each event, mentally complete the event in your mind. Schooling, a project, a goal, anything. You may use any method you choose, including imaginary "superpowers." After you have satisfactorily completed in your imagination, whatever it was you failed to do in the past, smile at it, mentally call it "completed," and go on to the next item. This healing of your past is a major mental benefit of the best and most powerful kind. At any time later, if you happen to think again of one of those "failures," smile at it, remind yourself that it is "completed," and move on. You're making "Who You Think You Are" **whole**. The part of our minds we are healing cannot tell the difference between a real event and an imagined event.

Exercise Number Four.

Enjoy another half hour of pleasure. Before you choose your pleasure exercise, think about the other five pleasure exercises already completed. Were they **fully** satisfying? Is there a way you can improve upon them the next time you treat yourself to a similar experience? In choosing this next exercise, make it **extra** special. Fulfill this exercise in the afternoon between the hours of one and six p.m. Begin by saying, "I, (your name), give myself permission to enjoy a half hour of pleasure." After the exercise is completed write a brief summary on the page headed "Pleasure Exercise Number Six."

Complete these exercises before going on to Chapter Seven.

"Pleasure Exercise Number Six"

____

Date Completed

Chapter Seven

All Of You

In the physical world,
certain metals can be joined together
to form a new metal
that's many times stronger
than the sum of their separate strengths.
It's called "alloying."
For example, suppose we take metal "A"
that has a tensile strength of four,
metal "B"
that has a tensile strength of two,
and metals C and D,
that each have a tensile strength of five.
Tensile strength is the metal's resistance
to lengthwise stress,
the ability of the metal to withstand
being pulled apart.
Adding their separate tensile
strengths together
we get a total of sixteen.
But when we combine these metals
and test the new product,
we find that a most magical
development has occurred -
the new product has a
tensile strength of one hundred!

The same type of magical development
happens to you
when all of your character attributes
are present and functioning at 100% capacity.
What are the character attributes that make up you?
Courage,
strength,
dignity,
honesty,
loyalty,
truthfulness,
responsibility,
trust,
tolerance,
capability,
compassion,
kindness,
consideration,
fairness,
morality,
and justice.
Look again at these attributes.
Briefly think about the meaning of each one.
Do that now.

Have you been using all those attributes
at your full capacity?
Say "yes" or "no" aloud,
so you can hear the answer.

Having heard your answer,
you should know
that you have limited yourself
to obtaining
only a small portion
of the terrific win
that's possible!

Your knowing *that you are a person*
who uses less than all your attributes
influences
"Who You Think You Are."
When you know that you are sometimes
less than fair,
less than considerate,
less than truthful,
less than kind,
less than moral,
less than courageous,
less than responsible,
less than loyal,
less than trustworthy,
in short, less than "whole,"
you have a diminished "self-image."

You project that self-image constantly.
It affects everything you say,
the way you carry yourself,
the way you look at people,
actually, all of your actions.
By functioning with less
than your full self,
you have done less, had less,
and been less
than was possible
had you been
functioning at full capacity.

Each time
you strengthen one of your character attributes
you become more capable
and more powerful.
Just as the armor of the knights of old
protected them when going into battle,
so your character attributes
are invincible shields—protecting you.
Think about the great personal benefits
that accompany a life of "wholeness,"
that go with being a person who projects
and attracts it.
When you bring 100% of yourself
into your daily life,
you create the finest circumstances possible,
which you then get to experience.

There's a popular children's song called
"The Hokey Poke."
The singers all join hands and form a circle.
Their actions follow the words of the song
which go something like this:
"You put your left foot in,
you put your left foot out,
you put your left foot in,
and you shake it all about."
Later on, you put in your right foot,
your right hand, and so on,
until finally your whole self is in.
Think about that song
the next time you consider your relationships with others.
How much of yourself do you want to put in?
Do you only put your left foot in
and then sit there wondering why you are getting less
from the relationship than you want?
Whatever *you bring to the game of*
"your life"
sets the limit
for how much you can get out.
To have what you want,
bring all that you have!

In a poker game where there is betting,
whether for money or match sticks,
you must put up an "ante."
The ante is the stake you put at risk
before you can get cards dealt to you.
The "limit" of the game
is the largest single bet
that a player can make at any one time.
In poker, the "limit" usually determines
what the "ante" is -
the higher the limit,
the higher the ante.
In your life,
it works the opposite way.
The "ante,"
what you bring to the game
determines what the "limit" is.
To have what you want,
up your personal ante!
Raise it to the maximum.
You choose
the game in which you play.

In upping your personal ante
you'll find that you move
from the "relative" or "almost" world
into the "100%" or "absolute" world.
Some examples of the 100% or absolute world are:
Arriving for your appointment on time,
speaking the truth,
starting a job and completing it,
and
making an agreement with someone and ***keeping*** *it.*
On the other hand,
some examples of the relative world are:
Almost in shape,
almost on time,
almost finished,
almost made it,
almost truthful,
almost a good friend,
almost a good partner,
almost a good mate,
almost,
almost,
almost.
An almost-made-it kind of existence.
In that world live second-rate relationships,
second-rate accomplishments,
and pure, bright human beings
acting the part of second-rate people.

I know you've made changes - major changes!
But you can make more!
You ***can*** *have what you want!*
Up your ante!
Bring ***all*** *of your honor to the game,*
all *of your capability,*
all *of your effort,*
all *of your courage,*
all *of your strength!*
"Now" is the only chance you have.
This *time called* ***"now"*** *is all you* ***ever*** *have.*
This *is your moment!*
This *is your chance to achieve greatness!*
How does one do it?
Up your personal ante!
Take off the limits!
Participate fully
with all you have.
That's *the way life is* ***meant*** *to be lived!*

What does life have to do with bits and pieces,
halves and partials?
Why muddy it,
halve it,
quarter it?
*Why leave part of **yourself** at home*
when you go out to play in the game of
*"**Your Life**"?*
Why play with others who have done the same?
***Every** action*
produces a result!
By living your life at less than 100% of your potential,
you severely limit
*what **you** can get from life.*
Up your personal ante!
Raise it to the maximum!
The rewards are colossal,
the players are terrific,
the game is exciting,
*and **you** are the winner!*

About a few of the attributes that make up you:

Courage and Fear

Courage and fear go hand in hand.
Courage is what you bring forth
to do the things you fear to do.
For courage to be necessary,
fear ***must*** *be present.*

Fear is your natural stimulus
that generates quick activity.
It causes adrenaline to be released into your system
for a quick power response.
In the middle of a street,
a car horn startles you -
you quickly jump back to avoid being hit -
fear,
in that case,
is your protector.
However,
like everything else,
it can have its negative side.
Many fears are born in your imagination
that have no basis in real life*.*

Put the book down for a moment
and carefully consider your concept of fear.
Do that now, before you read on.

Probably what you've thought of
is that fear involves "feeling afraid."
If you've focused only on the ***feeling****,*
which is the immediate ***effect*** *of fear,*
then look further for the complete answer.
"Feeling afraid"
only means that fear is present.
Beyond that immediate feeling of fear is -
your expectation
of a bad result.
If you were completely certain
that the situation would turn out perfectly,
actually, to your greatest benefit,
you would proceed with confidence.
On the other hand,
if you believe that a situation
will have a bad outcome,
your belief *produces fear.*
If the fear
is allowed to run through you,
without your courage awakening
in response to it,
then fear blocks your ability to act.

Where does the fear come from?
Is fear present within the situation itself?
Or is it generated within you?
For the answer, ask yourself,
"Who imagines the situation turning out badly?"

Do you let fear block you?
Or do you call upon your courage,
which then empowers you?
Fear can be a crippling emotion
but only if you fail to respond with courage.
You ***can*** *turn the situation into*
"just another work out situation."

The next time you feel fear
and there is time to think about the situation,
say the following things to yourself.

1. This is a work out situation.
2. This comes from the framework of my own life.
3. This is aimed at one of my weak areas.
4. It's aimed at that area so I can strengthen it.
5. There is some information I need
which I'll get by going through this situation.
6. I have enough courage to act
even though I'm afraid.
7. I'll feel good about myself
for having acted courageously.

Once you have made those seven statements,
imagine a beneficial outcome
rather than the one
that is causing your fear.
Then,
take action to handle the situation.

Strength

Your mental strength must be great
in order for you to persevere
in the face of all odds.
In every situation,
even the difficult ones,
your strength must carry you through
to the end.
***Only** when you cease your efforts*
to bring about a successful result
do you fail in your attempt.
As long as your effort continues,
in the end
*you **will** be successful.*

Truthfulness

Truth-fullness.
That means
all the truth - all the time.
The only reason you ever lied
was because you were afraid.
Fear again!
You knew what the truth was,
but you felt that if you told it,
you would experience a bad outcome.

You wanted to avoid that outcome,
so, in your mind,
you re-shaped what actually happened,
or was going to happen,
and told it in a way
that tricked your listener
into believing your new version.

Does distorting the truth change the reality of what is?
What really happened, still happened;
the ***real*** *past,*
which lives within you,
remains the same.
Your saying it differently
makes it more difficult to work with.
It's a seed you plant
in yourself
which you then have to carry around
while it grows.

If you are in a situation
where you feel you must lie,
use the same steps that you use
when you are confronted with a fearful situation.
They will bring about
the same freedom-producing results
because ***all*** *lying*
is based upon fear.

Telling the truth will bring you directness of mind
by eliminating falsehood.
The waste of energy and time
used in planning, executing, and maintaining a lie
will be eliminated from your life,
giving you back
your undivided, whole self.
Your future will be free
from waste and division.
You'll be complete
in your energy and attention.
You will enjoy ***straight*** *thinking*
and ***straight*** *talking,*
which will bring you ***straight*** *to your goals.*

Dignity

As your awareness and capability grow,
so grows your self-respect.
Self-respect can become a pitfall, though,
if it turns into overbearing swaggering.
Dignity is
self-respect at perfect pitch.
It's an internal trait that expresses
"Who You Are."
You walk into a room—confidently,
you meet the glance of others—directly,
in conversation,
your words are chosen—carefully.

Dignity and profanity are a poor mix;
the one cancels out the other.
Having dignity means
that you will refrain from doing certain things -
- things which would be out of character
for a person of noble ideals.
As your awareness and capability grow,
as you achieve dignity,
everyone you meet
will sense
"Who You Are"
and treat you accordingly.
It's a universal law -
- cause and effect.

Making It Yours

Exercise Number One.

Turn to the page in this chapter headed "Attributes Of a Whole Person." Look up the definitions of the words listed there. Write the definitions clearly for each word. Study the definitions until you feel you know, fully, what each one means and how it relates to you. Momentarily imagine yourself having each "attribute" and see how it feels. This imagining process is of great importance, so spend some time doing it well. Complete this first exercise before going on to the next exercise.

Exercise Number Two.

Find a quiet, comfortable place to sit. Turn to the page in this chapter headed, "Ways I Will Up My Personal Ante" and begin your list. Sign your name at the bottom of the page. Read your list every day for thirty days. Add items to it that you think of. Make one copy to carry, one copy for your mirror, one copy for your bathroom, and one copy for your favorite chair.

Your will
is the constant force
that will bring the items on your list into being.
Make it happen!

That is the way to strengthen yourself so you can live as a powerful, shining force. By your will power alone, you can raise your consciousness to the level where the things that you want "live." All you need to do is "up the ante." Be specific when you write the ways you will up your ante. If you write that you will bring more of yourself to a personal relationship, write **how** you will do that. If you resolve to do a job better, say **how** you are going to do it better - and then, follow through.

Exercise Number Three.

Think of a misrepresentation you have made to someone - a lie you've told. Before you read the next chapter, find the person or people and tell them the truth. It's hard! But remember - you are doing this for yourself! Also remember: you created this situation to work out on. This course of action is designed to make you into the kind of person you need to be to have what you want. Do it - and do it well! Do this exercise before going on..

Exercise Number Four.

Enjoy another half hour of pleasure. Begin by saying, "I, (your name), give myself permission to enjoy a half hour of pleasure." Choose a new pleasure exercise. Prepare for it; do what you can to make it extra nice. Make it a celebration of being here on earth. After the exercise is completed, write a brief summary on the page headed "Pleasure Exercise Number Seven."

Complete these exercises before going on to Chapter Eight.

"Attributes of a Whole Person"

Courage

Strength

Dignity

Honesty

Loyalty

Truthfulness

Responsibility

Trust

Tolerance

Capability

Compassion

Kindness

Consideration

Fairness

Morality

"Ways I Will Up My Personal Ante"

1.

Signature Date

"Pleasure Exercise Number Seven"

____

Date Completed

Chapter Eight

Commitment

In general usage, the word
"commitment"
is interchangeable with the word
"promise,"
and promises are sometimes broken.
On this path,
there is a special meaning for the word
"Commitment."
It means:
"That which is fulfilled."
From this time forward,
when you make a commitment,
what you are committed to is
"the same as done."

If,
***for any reason*,**
you fail,
then
what you thought was a commitment
was only a promise
or a plan -
- something you failed to do.
A commitment,
in the meaning that you and I now understand,
*is **always** fulfilled.*

It is essential
that you understand
the distinction between
"commitment"
and anything else
it is possible to fail in.

When you make a commitment,
understanding what it means,
the power to fulfill the commitment
arises
at the same time the commitment is made.
As you can see,
the ***making*** *of a commitment*
and
the ***fulfilling*** *of it*
are one and the same.

The workshops that I held were four weeks long,
five nights a week,
for one hour each night.
Twenty meetings
that spanned twenty-six days,
including weekends.
At the close of the first night's meeting,
everyone
who wanted to continue
was required to make a **commitment**
to be present at the remaining nineteen meetings
and
to be there **on time.**
If a participant failed
to appear on time
or missed a meeting,
for **any** *reason whatsoever,*
he or she had to drop out of the course
and wait for a new course to begin.
Some participants objected to this policy;
they said it overlooked
"valid reasons"
for being absent or late.
They failed to see that it was those same
"valid reasons"
that had given them the right to fail,
the right to have less than they wanted,
and the right to be powerless
up to that time in their lives.

In the workshops,
all *reasons for failing met the same fate.*
Only *those people who overcame* ***all*** *obstacles*
and came to ***every*** *meeting,* ***on time****,*
were at the final meeting.
They, too, had problems;
they, too, could have thought of
"valid reasons"
for coming late or missing a meeting,
and some of them encountered ***extreme*** *difficulty,*
but they chose to see it through,
overcoming ***everything*** *that came along.*
They had decided
they'd had enough of the way things were for them
and so they put forth
the ***necessary*** *effort*
to be at every meeting, on time.
They were committed.

The workshop participants made such incredible progress in their lives, and were so determined to fulfill their commitments, that some of them would leave their homes with enough time to spare that if their car broke down they could walk to the workshop.

Van, a workshop participant who had never been very successful in his life, failed to show up for a meeting. The next night he arrived at the workshop on crutches with a cast on his foot, and asked to be excused for his absence because he had broken his foot and had to go to the hospital to have the bone set. I refused. He became angry and said, "But, man, I **need** this workshop! I'm making the greatest progress of my life! A broken foot is a **valid** reason for missing a workshop. I replied that it was the "valid reasons" **that he had accepted** all his life that had always caused him to fail. I asked how he had gotten to the hospital. He said that a friend had driven him. I said that he could have had the friend drive him to the workshop and he could have gone to the hospital afterward. I said, "That's how a person who has made a commitment acts." He left angrily and never came back.

*Do you know **any** valid reason*
*for failing to live the life **you** want?*
*When you're **committed** to living*
the life of the aware and capable,
your need for
"excuses" and "reasons"
disappears.
*Success is the **only** road open to you.*

Sally, a workshop participant in her early forties, wanted very much to fulfill her commitment to be at all the workshop meetings, but she had a problem - several months before the workshop began, Sally had made a plan to go skiing with her family and friends. The date they had set turned out to be during the third week of the workshop, which was then in its second week. Sally told us she wanted to finish the workshop but that she had always been a weak person and her husband was very pushy. Sally said he was going to insist that she go as planned and she was afraid she would give in. I told her that all she needed was the absolute intention to fulfill her commitment to be present at all the remaining meetings of the workshop - that the capability, as well as the solution, was within her.

As the appointed day of departure neared, Sally became more and more nervous. She wanted to believe what I was telling her, yet she was still afraid she would give in to the pressure. She said her family was arguing with her every day about going. At the workshop, the night before the intended day of departure, we talked about it for the last time. All the other people in the workshop were giving her encouragement. I again told her that everything would turn out perfectly if she would only stick to her decision to fulfill her commitment. I told her this was an opportunity for her to take a giant step - a chance to break the control of those who were always deciding for her, against her will. The circumstances, coming from the framework of her own life, had brought about "the perfect next step" whereby she could achieve the strength she needed; all she had to do was call on her courage, face her situation, and come to the next workshop meeting.

The following night Sally was absent. When she returned from her skiing trip she telephoned and said she had waited for the solution to turn up "right until the last second" and then, because she failed to see any way out, she went on the trip.

Sally had "waited for the solution to occur," as if the "solution" had a mind of its own and was going to "happen" by itself. Who packed Sally's bags? Who walked out of Sally's house to the car? Who was it who went on the trip? Sally's "solution" was there all the time. She simply could have told her family that while she had made a **plan** to go skiing, she had made a **commitment** to complete the workshop. She could have told them that during her lifetime she had been a weak person and this was a wonderful opportunity for her to become strong and if her family would support her decision they would all benefit from it. She could have further said that the skiing trip would be over when they returned home but the benefits of her completing the workshop would go on and on. Her family, sensing her lack of true commitment had simply done what they had always done - bent her to their will. If she had been truly committed to completing the workshop, her family would have felt that absolute force; Sally would have had her way, overcoming their resistance and, thereby gained her much-needed freedom.

The way to perfect your ability
to make true commitments is clear:
Choose and act on a commitment.
Once you've made a commitment,
understanding all that it means,
you are a powerful person
and others must deal with you as such;
they will fail in trying to sway you;
they will fail in any attempt to divert you
from your chosen course of action.
By ***committing*** *yourself,*
in the true sense of the word,
you have already succeeded.

At the moment of true commitment
you are a source of great power.
How much?
As much as is needed to fulfill the commitment.
If you have any doubts or reservations,
if you have failed to be completely at one
with your commitment,
you will always be hesitant;
there will always be the lack of 100% effort
directed at a precise outcome;
there will always be less than complete effectiveness;
there will always be the possibility in your mind
that you can draw back.

That possibility will prevent you
from tapping your own strength
***fully*.**
When it comes to
"commitment"
there is only
one
possible outcome.

This is a black and white issue;
all the gray areas are gone.
There are few who speak of commitment
with the meaning that you now understand.
Nearly everyone accepts
indecision,
excuses,
weakness,
and reasons for failing;
nearly everyone
allows for the "gray" areas.
For the most part,
it's the gray areas that have regularly
"done you in"
all your life.
It's the gray areas that prevent you
from living in the world of the absolute
and keep you living in the relative world of
"almost" and "might have been."
In that world there are "acceptable" reasons for failing.

In the world of commitment,
failure is absent.
To exist there,
it is essential that you be able
to rely upon yourself,
fully.

When you fail to go forth ***resolutely****,*
you are ill-equipped
to deal with situations ***adequately****.*
Pay attention to the words
"resolutely" and "adequately."
They mean that if you want to have enough
of ***whatever it takes***
to fulfill your goal,
you have to commit yourself
to overcoming ***all*** *obstacles.*
When you have ***complete*** *determination,*
you go forth with the correct attitude,
which carries you through to your goal.
Everyone *stands aside to let a* ***determined*** *person go by.*

After you have come to the point of ***knowing***
you *can totally rely on* ***you****,*
you will radiate power
and great self-confidence.
Others will trust you
and ask you to be part of their plans.

You will be much sought after.
Promotions and opportunities of all kinds
will be offered to you.
People will know they can depend on you.
They will naturally trust your judgment and
your capability.
Your image will radiate control and
"doing-ness."
In your mind,
your range of achievable goals
will expand dramatically.
This will step up the whole process of changing
"Who You Think You Are"
into a new image of power and capability.

Imagine an archer about to shoot an arrow.
He stands with the bowstring fully drawn back,
the arrow pointed directly at its goal.
Now the archer looses the string
and in that moment of release.
the arrow speeds forward,
totally committed
to reaching its goal.
Imagine yourself as that arrow,
committed to absolutely reaching your goal,
acknowledging that you will overcome ***all*** *obstacles,*
that you will surmount ***all*** *problems,*
that you will,
under ***every*** *condition imaginable*
and beyond imagination,
attain *your goal.*

What that means is that
you will call upon ***every ounce of power***
and strength that you possess
in order to fulfill
that to which you have committed yourself.
When you set yourself to fulfill
projects,
goals,
and desires,
with that attitude,
obstacles and difficulties will dissolve
in the face of your total determination.

Making It Yours

Exercise Number One.

At this time, you are to think of something you want to do in your life - something that will be a **major** accomplishment for you. It might be straightening out, starting or ending a long term relationship. It might be changing jobs or leaving your home. Perhaps it is making a decision to marry or begin a partnership, or it might be the curing of a long illness. Perhaps it's learning a martial art or getting in top physical condition. It might be taking a long trip, starting a retirement path, or the fulfillment of a long awaited plan. Maybe it's ending financial or emotional dependence on someone. Whatever it is, **commit** to doing it now. Then, take the second step, which is to turn to the page in this chapter headed "My Commitment," and write down your commitment. Be clear and precise about what it is. Then, write the first steps that you will take in fulfilling your commitment. At this time, if you can only think of the first step, that is sufficient. Remember, while your goal is still far off you may only be able to see the first step in reaching it, but as you approach the goal the path becomes clearer, because what was at first far away, is now near. As you think of additional steps that will lead to your goal, add them to your list. As you accomplish steps on the way to your goal, check them off and write the date. Review your list every morning to see what you can do that day to move toward your goal, even though it might be only a small step. Review the list every night to see what you have accomplished that day and to plan for the next day. Each time you are able to cross off a completed step, you will feel a comforting sense of satisfaction, as well as being one step closer to accomplishing your goal.

If you need some assistance in knowing what steps to take in reaching your goal, imagine you are going on a journey. First, you need to decide where you are going, and what you want to do when you arrive. Then, you need to determine what needs to be done before you go. You'll also need to decide what you will want to take with you. It's the same when you make a commitment to accomplish a major goal. You decide what your goal is and what you need to do to accomplish it. Remember the old Chinese proverb: "even the longest journey ever made started with the first step." And the first step is **always** directly in front of you.

As soon as you have chosen your major goal, think of yourself as attaining it, **Act** as if you have attained it. The universe, being **required** to respond to you at **every** moment, will acknowledge your attainment.

Along the path to your goal you shall gain strength, wisdom, power, and happiness. In the end, you will discover that it was **the path** to your goal where life unfolded, and that it was the most important part of the journey, rather than reaching the goal itself. I wish you an exciting, fulfilling journey. If the major goal you choose is a true commitment for you, you will soon begin feeling the excitement that comes with attaining it.

Once you have decided on your major goal, made your written commitment to reach it, and listed the first steps needed to be taken in order to reach it, you may go on to the next exercise.

Exercise Number Two.

Enjoy another half hour of pleasure. Begin by saying, "I, (your name), give myself permission to enjoy a half hour of pleasure." Fulfill this exercise in the morning, sometime between the hours of 6 a.m. and 10 a.m., on any day you choose. If it is convenient, fulfill the exercise outdoors. After the exercise is completed, write a brief summary on the page headed "Pleasure Exercise Number Eight." Many years from now you will treasure your summaries.

Complete these exercises before going on to Chapter Nine.

"My Commitment"

Signature Date

“Steps To Take In Fulfilling My Commitment”

1.

Signature Date

“Pleasure Exercise Number Eight”

____

Date Completed

Chapter Nine

Saying It Positive

Many of the sentences you now say
are spoken in negative terms such as:
"I don't think I'll go,"
or,
"I don't think I want any of that."
But what does that mean,
"don't think"?
How do you go about "don't thinking"?
You can say it's just "a manner of speaking,"
however, the "manner" matters -
a lot.
***Everything** that you say*
*and **everything** that you do*
comes from your state of being
at the moment of saying or doing.
***Everything** that flows from you*
comes from who and what you are.
If you are angry,
you speak from your angry center;
your words are tinged with anger,
their meaning says anger.
When you think and speak negatively,
you produce negative results.
*Your "manner of speaking" **is** you.*

Negative statements have only a small amount of power
and even that small amount is present
only because the listener's mind
turns the statement around to its positive form.
An example of this is saying to someone,
"Don't go outside."
The listener's mind
automatically
turns that into its positive form:
"Stay inside."

To move away from negativity,
put substance into your words.
Instead of saying,
"I am not going to go,"
say what you ***are*** *going to do such as,*
"I am going to stay at home."
People need to have something substantial to react to.
If you speak negatively,
you can expect that often you will be
ignored
and
misunderstood,
and have only a small amount of influence.

To use an example,
suppose we were walking down a steep trail
with a sharp drop on one side
and I wanted to tell you,
"Watch where you're going."
Suppose I said it in its negative form -
"Don't watch where you're not going."
You would have to puzzle it out
and finally come to the conclusion
that if you are ***not*** *to watch where you're* ***not*** *going,*
then you ***are*** *to watch where you* ***are*** *going.*
Negatives are like that.

For your words to have power,
they must have direction and force:
"I am going to climb the mountain,"
"I am going to get the job,"
"I will win the prize."
What you could to say to someone is, for instance,
"Please go outside and play
rather than standing in front of me bouncing that ball.'
That's better than
"Don't do that!"
Give direction -
say what will be,
and it will be!

"Tried"
is another word of negativity
that works against you.
Used in the past tense,
it has **always** *meant that you failed.*
For instance, if you said,
"I tried to climb the mountain,"
you would have meant,
"I failed to climb the mountain."
If you had attempted to climb the mountain
and did it,
you would have said,
"I climbed the mountain."
If you had attempted to climb the mountain
and failed,
you would have said,
"I tried to climb the mountain,"
and then you would give the reason
why you failed to climb the mountain,
such as:
"I tried to climb the mountain but it was too steep,"
or,
"but it started to snow."

From this point forward, leave
"try"
out of your speech.
It's a word used to prepare for failure.
It's a way of excusing yourself
from doing the hard work of accomplishing
whatever it was you set out to do.
It gives you something to fall back on
in case of failure -
"I didn't say I **would** *do it,*
I said I'd **try** *to do it."*
It makes it a little easier to fail.

When you were a child,
perhaps you were brave enough to say,
"I am going to do this!"
Perhaps after having said that,
you made your brave attempt and failed,
and someone made fun of you because of it,
or you were made to pay some other price.
It only took you a short time
to learn that you had better be more careful
in how you spoke.
You learned to say,
"Well, I'm going to give it my best try,
but it's really tough,"
thereby providing an excuse to fall back on -
thereby preparing the way to failure.

By now, you've come to see failure
in the world around you
as an acceptable part of being human.
It's time to drop that belief.
***Trying** to do something is an admirable act;*
***finishing** it takes real courage.*
It takes a lot of courage to say,
"I will do it!"
meaning exactly that.
It's part of the path to having what you want.
It's perfectly all right to say,
"I will do it."
If you make your first attempt to do something
*and have a **seeming** failure,*
*as long as you are **in the process***
of fulfilling your intention
to do whatever it was you set out to do,
you are still on your way to achievement.
*The **only** time you fail*
is when you stop in your efforts
to accomplish your goal
with the intention of remaining stopped.
And when you say,
"At least I tried."
Those words signal your defeat.
Failure is partly the result of speaking in negative terms.
*It is **entirely** the result of thinking in negative terms.*

On the other hand,
the rewards for speaking in positive terms
are sensational.
The whole universe responds to you
with direct,
positive energy!
How else could it respond?
It is set up to react in a corresponding manner.
Your speech gives substance to your success.

By saying it positively,
you will find your thoughts clarified,
your speech direct,
the response of others rewarding.
You will have an ever-increasing command
over how life will be for you.
The positive power
of your words and intentions
will shape the future,
revealing the perfect place
that you are meant to naturally exist in.
Once you have mastered positive thought projection,
you will have attained great control over
"now,"
in its past, present, and future forms.

Making It Yours

Exercise Number One.

For the rest of today and all of tomorrow you are to speak in positive terms. Leave out all negative words such as "not" - can not, do not, will not. This is extremely hard. It is also extremely frustrating. Keep at it though, as the rewards are substantial. You will see to what extent you have learned to speak negatively by how hard it is to speak positively. It will take months, perhaps years of practice, before you begin to habitually speak positively. Today, you throw off more of the self-defeating beliefs that negativity and failure have any place in your speech or in your world.

Do whatever you need to do in order to keep up your level of awareness, such as carrying a small stone. Do **something** to keep yourself alert to what you are saying. If you are in conversation with someone for more than a few minutes, tell them about this exercise so they'll be patient with you while you find positive expressions for your thoughts.

When this task begins to look impossible, and it will seem that way, or when it becomes so frustrating you'd like to give it all up, remind yourself of the reasons why you have taken on this enormous task. To have come this far on the path is to be well along in achieving your goals and becoming the person you want to be.

Habit will cause you to say things in their negative form. Simply correct them and keep going. When you can say you have spent most of one day speaking positively you may consider the exercise accomplished. However, continue your efforts to speak positively, everyday, from now on.

Exercise Number Two.

Enjoy another half hour of pleasure. Begin by saying, "I, (your name), give myself permission to enjoy a half hour of pleasure." Fulfill this exercise in the evening between the hours of 6 p. m. and 11 p.m., on any day you choose. After the exercise is completed, write a brief summary on the page headed "Pleasure Exercise Number Nine."

Complete these exercises before going on to Chapter Ten.

“Pleasure Exercise Number Nine”

____

Date Completed

Chapter Ten

Giving Up Stress

When something important to you begins to
"go wrong,"
when your day and its plans seem to be
falling apart,
you may find yourself tempted
to question the perfection of your world.
When several such moments occur close together,
you may begin to feel tension.
It's worse when there are time factors involved.
By allowing this tension, or stress, to continue,
you insure its growing presence in your life.
Over a period of time,
stress can cause many physical ailments.

Seeing it phrased as,
"giving up stress"
should give you a good clue
as to how to eliminate it from your life.
You may have thought
that the exterior situations and events
which occur in your life
create stress.
As an aware person, you now know that
you
decide ***how***
you want to feel
about your situations.
If you remain
forever at the mercy
of the events that occur around you,
your stress level will go up and down
like a cork on the ocean.
Living a stress-free life
is a result of being knowledgeable, in control,
and practice - lots of practice.

It was about ten days into one of my workshops, when I arrived one evening to see a cluster of people standing around a new car talking excitedly. Later that evening, I congratulated the owner, Linda, on her new acquisition. I told her I had seen the car and its group of admirers outside. She said that what everyone was so excited about was not her car, but her reaction to its grille, which had been smashed that very morning! When she had first entered her apartment house garage that morning and seen the grille smashed, she had experienced a severe let-down. She had waited **so long** for her new car! But then, Linda suddenly remembered the workshop and looked at the smashed grille with new vision.

"Perfect!" she said, not believing it. "Perfect, that's just perfect."

She began to act and treat the situation, as though it were the best possible event that could have happened to her. Within a few moments, one of her neighbors who repairs cars appeared. (A gift from the Universe) He offered to assist her by giving her a good price for the repair and said he would do an excellent job. They took the car to his shop for an estimate and while she was there, she met some people who became interested in buying the product she sells in her business. The day was brightening! By the time Linda arrived at the workshop that evening, she was so exhilarated over her own response to the "mishap" that she was able to use it as a springboard to create excitement and enthusiasm in the group of people who had been around the car as I drove up.

Linda's enthusiasm and excitement came from her freedom from being at the mercy of the endless stream of seemingly unfortunate incidents which occur in everyday life. Before she acquired her attitude about events being "perfect," she said she would have spent the day feeling despondent and let-down. Linda said she might have gone back to bed to let the day pass before more bad things happened to her. But **that** day was different. That day she made into a kind of birthday—the first day of a new kind of life. Beginning that day, Linda was able to say **how** things were going to be for her, and how they're going to be is just perfect!

Take a moment now
and imagine what it would mean for you
to be free
from the bad side effects
that result from the seemingly unfortunate mishaps
which regularly occur in your life.
If you fail to realize
that you are in charge of your reactions
*and that **how** you react **contributes***
to the creation of the immediate future,
you will continue to create
many stressful hours for yourself.
When a seemingly bad event occurs,
see it as though it were a good event,
the best possible event.
*Treating it that way is a **major** step*
in giving up stress.

In the beginning,
you may have to pretend
that difficult events are perfect.
When you are able to naturally react
as though everything were for your benefit,
that's when life becomes nice.

As the continuing parade of events
passes through your life,
be like a mountain -
while the storms come and go,
the winds blow,
the sun shines,
and the events occur,
the mountain remains solid and calm.

Do you spend time regretting the events of the past,
saying to yourself,
"If only it could have been different,"
or, "If only I would have done this instead of that,"
or, "I wish that wouldn't have happened?"
When you think about the way things
should have been
or could have been,
but weren't,
you're creating stress for yourself.
You're also creating unhappiness for yourself.

I had a friend, Frank, who died a few years ago. Many times during the thirty-year period we knew each other he said to me, "I sure wish I had gone to college! That was the biggest mistake I ever made, not going to college." Just after Frank graduated from high school, he had the opportunity to begin college but instead he went to work as a laborer. For thirty-odd years he regretted his choice. What he liked to say was, "If only I had gone to college, things would be different for me now." He paid a price by thinking he had made a mistake when he chose to go to work rather than go to college. Frank continued to pay the same price over and over during all those thirty years. Whenever there was bad weather and he had to go to work, he would say, "If only I had gone to college I wouldn't have to be working outside in the rain today," and he would again regret his decision. Frank mentally beat himself up like that for all those years. I never once heard him say, "Gee, this is such a great day today and I get to work outside." Frank saw only the negative side of his situation. Neither did he take any action to remedy the situation and go to college.

Events are just events;
how you react to them
determines
how they continue to affect you.
Part of learning how to give up stress
is understanding that
when an event becomes reality,
*it was the **only** possibility.*
To clarify that, I'll say it in the following way:
Given all that went before -
and all that did not go before -
what happened was the only possibility.

Here's an exaggerated, imagined example to make that point. Let's say at the beginning of last spring you decided that you would like to have tomatoes grow in your back yard. Here are a few of the things that **did** happen. You got the idea to plant tomatoes, you went to the store and bought tomato seeds, you came back home, you got out the gardening tools, you went into your back yard, you prepared the soil, you put the seeds in, you covered the seeds with soil, you wet the soil, and in the weeks that passed the sun shone and you continued to provide water and food for the tomato plants. In time, they matured and produced an abundance of tomatoes.

Here are some of the things that did **not** happen. You did not get an idea to plant corn instead of tomatoes. You went to the store and did not buy pumpkin seeds by mistake. You did not go on a long vacation rather than going back home with the tomato seeds. Upon arriving home, you did not get a grinder from the shed and grind the tomato seeds into pulp. You did not plant the seeds in cement rather than soil. You did not leave the seeds uncovered so the birds could eat them. In fact, a bird did not come and eat them. You did not drown the seeds with water. During the weeks that passed a garbage truck did not drive over your seeds and smash them into the earth, neither did a plane crash on your tomato plants as they were growing, nor did the bugs come and eat your plants, nor did an earthquake occur which opened a crevice under your plants and swallow them into the ground. These are just some of the many things that did not happen. As you can imagine, the list of things that did **not** happen is truly endless. So: "Given all that **did** happen and all that did **not** happen, what finally happened was the **only** possibility."

Once an event has occurred,
your job is to look at it
as being ***the only event that was possible****.*
If there were people involved
who ***seemed*** *to have had several choices open to them,*
realize that
whatever *choice they made*
was ***their only choice possible****.*
You may find this difficult to agree with
because it
seems
as if they had several choices available.
But that is the main point:
When you take into consideration
all *the factors involved in the situation,*
what did and did not happen,
the choice they made was ***the only one possible****.*

You may find yourself saying to someone,
"You could have done that differently," or,
"You didn't have to say that," or,
"Why didn't you do this instead of what you did?"
Saying those kinds of things creates stress.
When you're arguing with someone
about the way something could have been done
or should have been done,
realize that the person
was only capable of doing it
in the one way he or she did it.

It is also the same for all the things
***you** have done*
*in **your** lifetime.*
The events of the past,
which continue to make you feel badly,
*were the **only** events that could have possibly occurred,*
given all that went before
and all that did not go before.

If you could go into the past
and return to an event that occurred in your life,
one that you regret,
and if you could relive that event
and what led up to it,
second by second,
*knowing **all** the elements*
that went into creating the event
and your decision to do
whatever you did
or did not do,
you would clearly see
at the end of your journey
that what happened was
the only possibility.

In order for you to give up stress,
stop punishing yourself, and others,
for "wrong doings" and "mistakes" of the past.
When you think about events of the past
that cause you stress today,
recognize that they were perfect events,
events that could only have occurred in the way they did.

If you would like to bring
pleasant, beneficial times
into your life,
learn to take the stress out of events
that happen in your life
and in the lives of others.
When your friends, mate,
or acquaintances
do something that seems wrong,
let them know that it is
"All right."
Do it in a way which lets them know that you mean it.
A good way to begin is by saying
"It's all right."
Then you might continue
by explaining that your personal philosophy
causes you
to believe that when an event occurs
it's for everyone's complete benefit.

It might take a little time for everyone
to see that it was just right,
but, in the meantime, you have treated it
in a way that lets you experience
the good feelings and good effects
that come from that type of action.
If what the person did
was not what you wanted,
you might want to say to him or her
that if a similar event occurs in the future
you would like it handled it in a different way,
and you could describe what that different way is.
In that manner you will bring the greatest benefits
to the lives of all those you come in contact with
and the greatest benefits to yourself.

Giving up stress will smooth out your life
and bring harmony to your environment.
When a master passes through an area of conflict,
there is a space of peace and harmony
surrounding the master;
"Who The Master Is"
affects all who are near.

A samurai warrior, a violent man, approached a great Zen master and said, "Is there a heaven and a hell? And if so, teach me of them!" The master replied, "What would a stupid Samurai warrior like yourself do with such knowledge?" The enraged warrior drew his sword, and, with a ferocious yell, was sending it on its way to cleave off the master's head when the master held up his hand and cried, "Open here the gates of hell!" The Samurai stopped his sword, realizing the great teaching, and how the master had offered himself to give it. It became crystal clear to him what "hell" was, and he was overwhelmed with respect for the master. He dropped his sword and bowed low to the master. The master spoke again, "Open here the gates of heaven!" At this, the Samurai gave up his warlike ways and became a student of the Zen master.

"Who The Master Was"
made such an impression on the warrior
that, in an instant,
he was transformed.
"Who You Are"
also transforms others
and the world around you -
constantly.
It has always been that way.
Do it now
in the full awareness
that it ***is*** *happening*
and that it is ***you***
who is doing it.

Is it tough to keep aware?
It's the most difficult job I know.

If
you could choose
to see the events of the past, present, and future
as being ***completely*** *beneficial*
would stress disappear?
Is *the choice yours?*

Making It Yours

Exercise Number One.

Turn to the page at the end of Chapter Three headed "My Philosophy." It reads:

"Every event that occurs is for my greatest benefit."

Change the period at the end of the sentence to a dash and add: "and is the only event possible." Your finished sentence should read:

"Every event that occurs is for my greatest benefit - and is the only event possible."

Exercise Number Two.

Find a quiet place where you can be alone and undisturbed for an hour. Sit quietly and go back over the events of your life starting from the time you were a small child. As you come forward in time, recall those times when you did something that was hurtful to another. As you recall each incident, see it as "perfect." Mentally, call it "perfect," even though you may still believe the person was actually hurt by your actions. Realize that, given all that went before and all that did not go before, what happened was the only possibility. Even though, in the beginning, you may fail to see why the event was beneficial in the other person's life, heal your past by calling the event "perfect." Use all your new-found knowledge to see it that way. You may complete this exercise in two sessions of a half-hour each, but make sure they are a full half-hour. During the time you are searching through your memory for hurtful events, if your mind wanders to other kinds of events which you spend time thinking about, estimate the time so spent and add it to your session. If you need more than one hour, take it, or add additional sessions. You are a pure, bright spirit, here to gain the experiences of this lifetime; each experience is necessary, each experience takes you to the next level of awareness.

Since part of **every** person is the sum total of all that has gone before in his or her life, your taking this time to perfect all that has gone before in your life is an exercise of major importance. Do it well and to your complete satisfaction.

Exercise Number Three.

Enjoy another half hour of pleasure. Before choosing your pleasure exercise, think about the other nine exercises that you have already completed. Pick out the moments when you experienced the most satisfying sense of pleasure - the moments that you relive with the greatest satisfaction. In choosing this pleasure exercise let yourself be guided by those special moments. Begin by saying, "I, (your name), give myself permission to enjoy a half hour of pleasure." After the exercise is completed, write a brief summary on the page headed "Pleasure Exercise Number Ten."

Complete these exercises before going on to Chapter Eleven.

"Pleasure Exercise Number Ten"

____

Date Completed

Chapter Eleven

The Price of Failure
The Price of Success

Let's talk first about the price of failure.
You know it means losing,
but what else?
Put the book down for a moment and think of five things
that come under the heading of
the price you pay for failure.
Write them down
on the page at the end of this chapter headed
"The Price Of Failure."
Do that now, before reading on.

Perhaps failing to have enough money
prevents you from fulfilling many desires.
Perhaps you fail in being able to do what you want to do.
What about loss of self-respect
and loss of respect from others,
especially your family and friends?
What about disillusionment,
loss of happiness,
and the inability to go where you want,
when you want,
how you want,
and with whom you want?
What about lacking the possessions you want?
The price of failure is mighty high.

If you can,
think of five items
that come under the heading of
the price you pay for success.
Write down the ones you can think of
on the page at the end of this chapter headed
"The Price Of Success."
Do that now.

If you had difficulty in thinking of five items
for the price you pay for success
it would be quite natural.
If there is a price one pays for success,
it is beyond my knowledge.
In all the workshops I have given,
I always asked this question
about the price of success.
I have yet to hear an answer that seems fitting.
The usual answer is "hard work,"
but on the road of success,
hard work is actually a benefit rather than a loss.

An answer someone might give would be:
"In order to be financially successful,
I have paid the price of having to be away
from my family and friends
while I was battling it out on the business scene."
That's a price of failure -
failure to be able to earn a living in a way
that enables that person to also spend time
with his or her family.
Any "price" you feel you may have paid
for achieving any type of success,
financial or otherwise,
was really a price of failure.
Even though the ultimate goal is finally achieved,
the "price" you paid in achieving it
was a price you paid for failing -
failing to be able to do it in a way
that allowed you to be successful
***all along the way**.*
Look at the items you wrote down
as being the price of success.
Are they the price of success or of failure?

The legendary Chinese sage, Lao Tzu,
said about the person
who has made it in life,
"He has his yes, he has his no."
He meant that for the knowledgeable, capable person,
"no" ***results*** *in a no,*
"yes" ***results*** *in a yes.*
It means being in charge.
It means getting to say
how it's going to be for you -
how it **is** *for you.*

Once you have merged
the concepts of this path into your mind,
your road ***to*** *success*
will actually be
your road ***of*** *success.*
Having the knowledge
that you ***will*** *reach your goal*
means you are ***already*** *a success.*
When you have this knowledge,
your actions radiate success.
All who come in contact with you
experience the successful person you ***are****.*
Goals are then achieved quickly
and advances come rapidly.
When a ***seeming*** *setback comes,*
you will look at it
as one of the ***necessary*** *occurrences*
on the way to your successful goal,
part of the success
rather than the unfortunate mishap
it ***appears*** *to be.*
When you fully realize
that your goal is ***attained***
once you have ***committed*** *yourself to*
achieving it,
then what becomes most important
is ***the path*** *to your goal -*
that's where life unfolds
in its moment-by-moment wonderment.

Several years ago, I paid a visit to the London offices of a film distributor. I was there to talk to the managing director about the distribution of my one-third finished film. He told me his company would only consider signing a contract to distribute a film after the film was completed and they had seen the finished product.

"Oh, that's good," I said, "then this will be the first time."

"No, it won't be the first time," he replied, "we just don't do it."

Eight weeks later the contract was signed. Eight weeks was the time this man needed to get used to the idea of a change in policy. I was patient and persevering; I knew from the beginning what the outcome would be and I had already experienced the success of the achievement. I didn't know how long it would take, but I knew there were reasons I had to be in London. I didn't know what the reasons were, but I knew that I would find out while I finished the negotiations with the managing director. And I knew that what was important for me was what else would happen during the time of the negotiations.

There may be things in your life
which you think have been,
or are currently,
detrimental to your happiness
or to your success.
Perhaps you think your read poorly
or that in conversation
you're less than a dazzling wit,
less than an audience-charmer.
Perhaps you think your looks
leave something to be desired
or that your personality is unexciting.
Maybe you have a physical impairment,
perhaps you're poor,
perhaps you have only a small amount of formal education,
or perhaps in school you are, or were,
less than a brilliant student.

Perhaps at work there are others
who seem to get ahead faster than you
and you feel that you could, too,
if only you "knew" someone.
After all, you've heard the old saying:
"It's not what you know, it's who you know."

If any or all of these feelings and situations
exist in your life,
this is the time for you to realize
that those supposed handicaps
are a benefit to you.
If you think that you have to become a success
"in spite of them"
rather than "because of them,"
you will forever wander around,
looking for success,
thinking that you are being held back
by the very things that have ***perfectly*** *equipped you*
to achieve ***any*** *goal you desire!*

One day I received a letter from a person who had heard an interview I gave on the radio and he wrote:

"Hello, my name is Cory. I heard your radio program and was thrilled by it! I, too, used to look at life in much the same way that you do today. I, too, believed that I could have anything I wanted. I was capable and powerful and everything was going my way, until I suffered a great tragedy. It is so humiliating, I cannot even tell you about it, not even in a letter. It changed my whole life. I am a recluse now and I sit at home much of the time hoping that no one will find out my secret. I used to have many friends and was considered quite a man-about-town. That has all changed - since the terrible event came into my life four years ago, everything has gone wrong; it has left me powerless. I am too embarrassed to tell you what the event was, even though you don't know who I am and will never know who I am. I want very much to come and take your workshop but I cannot do that. You see, I want to be a star, a movie star. I know I have it in me to be that star and if I were to come and take your workshop now and tell you what my terrible secret is, then, when I became a star, you would know my secret and I wouldn't be able to stand the shame of it. I am asking you to give me your workshop over the telephone. I will pay whatever you ask, but my identity must remain a secret. I am a nobody now, but one day I will be a somebody and my secret must remain safe."

I wrote to Cory and said that he could come to the workshop and **keep** his secret. He called me on the phone and said that he didn't want to do that.

"Cory, you tell me that you are going to be a great star **in spite of** your great handicap. As long as you continue in that line of thinking, the chances of your becoming a great star are incredibly slim. On the other hand, if you knew that you could become a star **because** of your handicap, then your chances would immediately increase a hundredfold. If you knew that everything that has occurred in your life to this point, including this telephone call, has equipped and prepared you for the stardom you desire, you would be looking at your `hardship' with new eyes, **knowing** that it was an essential part of your stardom. Further, if you knew that all things are possible for those who believe that all things are possible, you would be a star already. Everyone who has that knowledge is already a super star. What happened in your life is beyond recall because you are unable to roll back time to do it in another way. What you **can** do is to change the way you look at the event. Treat what happened as the best thing that could have happened - make believe it happened **so that you may become a star**! After all, since it has occurred, that's the only rational option you have if you wish to be successful. If you continue to look at what happened as a detriment in your life, an obstacle, that's what it will continue to be. You can change the way you think about it at any moment, including this one. By making a big, bad thing out of what happened and by keeping it a secret, you increase the negative power of the event. What happened to you may be very powerful, but you are using its power in a way that works against you and holds you back rather than propelling you forward. Should you achieve stardom, **it will be because of what happened to you."**

It's important to remember
that the universe you live in is set up
so that everything benefits you completely.
Whatever has happened to you,
whatever you are,
whatever you have been,
whatever you have,
is exactly what you need
in order to become anything
and everything you want.
The only thing you need to do is
act on it!

In the olden days, there was a great prince who was leading his followers against a horde of invaders who threatened his little kingdom. One of the prince's soldiers, a young captain, looked enviously over at the prince who was holding his golden sword aloft, it's blade flashing in the sun, and he said to himself, "If I had a sword like that, I too could lead this charge, but all I have is this plain blade!" And so saying, he angrily snapped his weapon in half across his knee, flung it away from him, and crept off the field. Later in the day, the prince, who had lost his sword in battle, was being driven back by the invaders. As he came upon the spot where the deserting captain had flung his broken sword, he saw it lying in the sand! With a glad cry, he leaped off his horse, grabbed up the broken sword, and with it, turned and led the charge, achieving a great victory!

Have you paid the price of failure long enough?
Have you worked at a job that is less than you want
long enough?
Have you shared a relationship with your mate
that has been less than fulfilling
long enough?
Have you been experiencing mediocre friendships
long enough?
Have you been less than a good student
long enough?
Have you been less of the person you know you can be
long enough?

One day, when I had come to see the managing director of the film distribution company in England, I struck up a conversation with a young woman who worked there as a typist. She told me she wanted to be a ballerina. I asked her what she was doing working as a typist and she replied that she was earning money to take ballet lessons.

"Why not just go and study with a ballerina?"

"I need to earn the money to pay for the lessons."

"Well," I said in a deliberately offhand manner, "I suppose being a ballerina means very little to you."

"Oh no! That's not true. I want to be a ballerina more than anything in the whole world!"

"If that's true, you may begin to take ballet lessons immediately."

"Oh no! Ballet lessons are very expensive and there is only one woman I want to study under!" She named a great prima ballerina who was then teaching in London.

"Look, if you will do what I say, you may begin taking lessons from this wonderful teacher immediately."

I told her she was to find the ballet teacher that very day and tell the teacher that she wanted, more than anything else in the whole world, to be a ballerina. She would do anything that the ballet teacher asked, if only she could study with her. She would wash floors, mend costumes, work on the sets, do any kind of job at all, so long as she could study with the great dancer. She would also study hard and practice everyday, if only she could have the opportunity to dance. Although she was a bit uncertain at first, after we had talked a while more, she agreed to do as I said.

The next morning, when I walked into the office, girl came over to me and her eyes filled with tears as she said, "It's all true!"

The power
to reach your goals
lives within you.

Remove the limitations you have accepted
and you will be drawn to your goals
as a stone is drawn to the bottom of a pool.
If you say
this plan
or that idea
can only fail -
the failure you predict
is yours.

You began this path because what you had
was different from what you wanted
and you decided to change that!
Well, make the change
completely!
Carry this book in your hands
until it is in your mind!
Overcome all that has gone before!
Up the ante!
You are in control!
You are the center from which everything radiates!

I know how hard this is for you.
You're like a new blade of grass
pushing against the earth,
struggling to make its way into the light.
Perhaps there is even a small stone
right over the spot where you want to emerge!
Supreme effort is required!
The reward is a life in the sun!

The price of failure is too high to pay.
The benefits of success are too great to pass by.
***This** is your time for being strong and persevering.*
*The power **is** within you!*
*The will **is** within you!*
***All** your effort must be concentrated on persevering.*

How about this:
A driveway nearby
was recently resurfaced
with two inches of blacktop.
Three weeks later,
a blade of grass pushed its way through.

Making It Yours

Exercise Number One.

Get a dictionary and look up the word "persevere." Do this even if you know the definition. Then, turn to the page in this chapter headed "Persevere," and write down the definition. Under the definition write, "**I will persevere**." Underline each of the three words separately and then sign your name. Write the words with conviction, with power, and with the full force of your will.

Exercise Number Two.

You are to find a person who needs encouragement and information of the kind you are now able to give and assist that person in discovering the concepts you now know. Tell that person that you are doing it as part of a path.

A good way to begin is to read from the beginning of this book to the end of Chapter One, taking notes. Use your notes to begin assisting the other person. Tell them that they could help you by agreeing to let you share this path with them. It will be a valuable experience for both of you and you will be "Making It Yours" in the most powerful way possible. Do it well and to your complete satisfaction. Avoid the attitude, "I know more than you do." Your assistance may be required for a long while but as long as you continue to share your knowledge, you will grow in awareness and capability. It is only necessary that you **begin** to assist the person before going on to Chapter Twelve.

Exercise Number Three.

Sit quietly for a half hour and think of things about yourself that you believe are detrimental, things that you think are holding you back. As you remember each item, smile at it; realize it is essential for it to be present in your life. Realize that you need to have the experience of dealing with it. Realize it was one of the essential ingredients that has enabled you to arrive at this point in time, where you can have what you want. Keep at it until you can use what you previously considered as a fault as a springboard for achievement. Should you fail to be able to see these seeming faults as being beneficial, read this chapter again and then sit down and evaluate the items once more.

Exercise Number Four.

Enjoy another half hour of pleasure. Fulfill this exercise with another person. Be creative, prepare for the occasion thoughtfully, and include a person of your choice in making the plan. Discuss it with them to see if they can add to the enjoyment. After the exercise is completed, write a brief summary on the page headed "Pleasure Exercise Number Eleven."

Complete these exercises before going on to Chapter Twelve.

“The Price of Failure”

“The Price of Success”

"Persevere"

Definition:

Signature　　　　　　　　Date

“Pleasure Exercise Number Eleven”

____

Date Completed

I am interested in knowing who you are. When you have a spare moment, drop me note and tell me a little about yourself, what you do to earn a living, what you like to do, what your achievements have been, what your regrets are, what you hope for yourself, and things of that nature. You can write to me in care of Power Press at the address in the front of this book. Thank you.

Respectfully,

-wu wei

Chapter Twelve

Of Maximum Importance

You are nearing the end of the book now.
There's only a little way to go.
We have been together
just for the time it has taken you
to progress to this point.

Having come so far,
you have my complete congratulations.
The path you have followed is a solitary path
and a difficult one.
As you continue to follow this path,
merging more of the book's concepts into yourself,
you will become ever more aware,
ever more capable.

Of maximum importance
is that you keep aware
of your personal philosophy.
It will serve you well
through your lifetime.

Of maximum importance
is that you keep aware
that an event,
in itself,
is only an event.
How you respond to it
determines what it becomes for you.
To say that it was perfect,
to treat it that way,
to recognize that it was the only possibility,
will keep you experiencing the best of all possible worlds.

Of maximum importance
is that you keep aware
that all of life is a mirror.
"Who you are"
is reflected there.
If you are dissatisfied with the reflection,
make an inner change that will cause the Universe to
respond to you in a different way.

Of maximum importance
is that you keep aware
that circumstances come into your life
so that you can work out on them
and thereby
become more aware
and more capable.
Confront them.
Handle them.
Remember,
when the path gets tough,
you're still on the right track,
just a tough track.

Of maximum importance
is that you keep aware
that you are unique in this world -
one of a kind.
Everything *that you perceive*
is different for you
than it is for everyone else.
What's true for you
may be true only for you -
what's true for another
may fail to be true for you.

Of maximum importance
is that you keep aware
that you are the center of your personal universe
affecting everyone and everything around you.

Of maximum importance
is that you participate in life
*with **all** you have.*
Remember, when all the attributes
that make up you are in place
and operating at peak capacity,
you have "alloyed" yourself,
armored yourself,
and are of awesome capability.

Of maximum importance
is your knowledge
that all things are possible for you,
who believe that all things are possible.
You now know
that you are a person who achieves results.
When you have decided on a course of action,
if it suits your preference to continue on that course,
*you **will** be successful.*

Of maximum importance
is that you remember
that the power to fulfill ***every*** *commitment*
arises within you.
You are a person
capable of true commitment.

Of maximum importance
is that you remember
that an end, in itself,
is only a symbol of completion.
It is this path that you follow to reach that end
where life unfolds,
where capability grows,
where knowledge is gained,
and where happiness is found.

Of maximum importance
is that you keep aware
that all of life is a path.
Your desires and your circumstances
will lead you along that path.
Circumstances will force you in a particular direction
so that your awareness and capability
can grow in a needed way.
Following your desires,
you will discover an inner well of joy.

Of maximum importance
is that you continue
to create pleasure for yourself.

Of maximum importance
is that
when you remember a hurtful incident from the past
done either to you or by you,
you immediately heal it
by acknowledging it's perfection
for yourself and for everyone else.
Remember the absolute test
to determine if something is perfect:
If it happened, it is.

Of maximum importance
is that you keep aware
that everything is exactly as it should be -
and for your best benefit.
It might be
that you will want to make changes
in the way things are -
that's exactly right, too.

You have broken loose
from that which bound you.
You are a shining, radiant being,
gifted with the powers of the universe
in this wondrous moment called now,
which is the only time that ever is.

It is refreshing to look at the evening sky
and see perfection.
It is wonderful to look at a vast mountain range
or a great ocean
and see perfection,
and yet, in addition to those things,
there are these:

All the events in your life
that have brought you to this moment
are perfect;
your being where you are is perfect;
your reading this is perfect
and
***you** are perfect.*

-wu wei

Making It Yours

Exercise Number One, The Final Exercise

Throughout this path, you have learned how to create the world around you and how to obtain what you want. However, all that has gone before in your life has consumed a **vast** amount of time in comparison to the **little** amount of time you have spent with me walking the path. I have seen, from careful observation of people on the path, that unless guidance, inspiration, and encouragement **continue** on a **daily** basis, the past history of the individual clouds their awareness, undermines their gains, and claims their "now." This path, to be completely effective, goes on as long as you are alive.

It is **essential** that you nourish yourself **each day** with the concepts in this path. Therefore, beginning tomorrow, for the next 365 days, read this book for three minutes each day. Begin at Chapter I. At the end of each day's reading, **mark your place** so you will know where to begin the next day. **Keep the concepts alive.**

I recommend, if you have not already done so, that you purchase I Ching Wisdom, Volumes I and II, and read a page or two a day. I also recommend, if you have not already done so, that you obtain a copy of The I Ching, and fifty yarrow stalks, and that you use them to obtain guidance. If you have any questions, please direct them to me in care of Power Press, whose address, telephone, fax, and email address are at the front of this book. Do not be hesitant, it is my honor to be of assistance to you.

I wish you the greatest of good fortune.

—wu wei